Student Language Scale

Nickola Wolf Nelson, Ph.D., CCC-SLP, BCS-CL
Barbara M. Howes, Ph.D., LMSW
Michele A. Anderson, Ph.D., CCC-SLP

I0737590

TILLS™
TEST OF INTEGRATED LANGUAGE & LITERACY SKILLS™

This Student Language Scale may be used with the Test of Integrated Language and Literacy Skills™, other assessment tests, or as a stand-alone measure to gather multiple perspectives on a student's language/literacy abilities and other skills.

Student's name: ____________________ Grade: __________ Date: __________

Person responding: ☐ General education teacher ☐ Special education teacher ☐ Other: __________
☐ Student ☐ Parent/guardian

RATING SCALE

Compared with other students of the same age, circle the number to show how good this student is at...	**Not good**						**Very good**
1. Understanding school vocabulary words	1	2	3	4	5	6	7
2. Using school vocabulary words when talking	1	2	3	4	5	6	7
3. Figuring out new words when reading	1	2	3	4	5	6	7
4. Spelling words correctly when writing	1	2	3	4	5	6	7
5. Understanding a story when listening	1	2	3	4	5	6	7
6. Telling a story that makes sense	1	2	3	4	5	6	7
7. Understanding a story when reading	1	2	3	4	5	6	7
8. Writing a story that makes sense	1	2	3	4	5	6	7
9. Following spoken directions	1	2	3	4	5	6	7
10. Being organized about schoolwork	1	2	3	4	5	6	7
11. Paying attention in school	1	2	3	4	5	6	7
12. Interacting socially with other students	1	2	3	4	5	6	7

ABILITY CHECKLIST

Please check the things that you think are **easiest** for this student to do:

☐ Art (drawing/painting) ☐ Dance ☐ Music ☐ Mechanical ☐ Sports ☐ Math ☐ Social ☐ Listening ☐ Talking
☐ Reading ☐ Writing ☐ Other: __________

Comments:

Please check the things that you think are **hardest** for this student to do:

☐ Art (drawing/painting) ☐ Dance ☐ Music ☐ Mechanical ☐ Sports ☐ Math ☐ Social ☐ Listening ☐ Talking
☐ Reading ☐ Writing ☐ Other: __________

Comments:

PRIORITY QUESTION

What one thing do you think is most important to help this student do better at school?

P2010301

Student Language Scale

SLS

TILLS™ TEST OF INTEGRATED LANGUAGE & LITERACY SKILLS™

Nickola Wolf Nelson, Ph.D., CCC-SLP, BCS-CL
Barbara M. Howes, Ph.D., LMSW
Michele A. Anderson, Ph.D., CCC-SLP

This Student Language Scale may be used with the Test of Integrated Language and Literacy Skills™, other assessment tests, or as a stand-alone measure to gather multiple perspectives on a student's language/literacy abilities and other skills.

Student's name: ______________________ Grade: __________ Date: __________

Person responding: ☐ General education teacher ☐ Special education teacher ☐ Other: __________
☐ Student ☐ Parent/guardian

RATING SCALE

Compared with other students of the same age, circle the number to show how good this student is at...	**Not good**						**Very good**
1. Understanding school vocabulary words	1	2	3	4	5	6	7
2. Using school vocabulary words when talking	1	2	3	4	5	6	7
3. Figuring out new words when reading	1	2	3	4	5	6	7
4. Spelling words correctly when writing	1	2	3	4	5	6	7
5. Understanding a story when listening	1	2	3	4	5	6	7
6. Telling a story that makes sense	1	2	3	4	5	6	7
7. Understanding a story when reading	1	2	3	4	5	6	7
8. Writing a story that makes sense	1	2	3	4	5	6	7
9. Following spoken directions	1	2	3	4	5	6	7
10. Being organized about schoolwork	1	2	3	4	5	6	7
11. Paying attention in school	1	2	3	4	5	6	7
12. Interacting socially with other students	1	2	3	4	5	6	7

ABILITY CHECKLIST

Please check the things that you think are **easiest** for this student to do:

☐ Art (drawing/painting) ☐ Dance ☐ Music ☐ Mechanical ☐ Sports ☐ Math ☐ Social ☐ Listening ☐ Talking
☐ Reading ☐ Writing ☐ Other: __________

Comments:

Please check the things that you think are **hardest** for this student to do:

☐ Art (drawing/painting) ☐ Dance ☐ Music ☐ Mechanical ☐ Sports ☐ Math ☐ Social ☐ Listening ☐ Talking
☐ Reading ☐ Writing ☐ Other: __________

Comments:

PRIORITY QUESTION

What one thing do you think is most important to help this student do better at school?

Student Language Scale

SLS

TILLS™ TEST OF INTEGRATED LANGUAGE & LITERACY SKILLS™

Nickola Wolf Nelson, Ph.D., CCC-SLP, BCS-CL
Barbara M. Howes, Ph.D., LMSW
Michele A. Anderson, Ph.D., CCC-SLP

This Student Language Scale may be used with the Test of Integrated Language and Literacy Skills™, other assessment tests, or as a stand-alone measure to gather multiple perspectives on a student's language/literacy abilities and other skills.

Student's name: ______________________ Grade: __________ Date: __________

Person responding: ☐ General education teacher ☐ Special education teacher ☐ Other: __________
☐ Student ☐ Parent/guardian

RATING SCALE

Compared with other students of the same age, circle the number to show how good this student is at...	**Not good**						**Very good**
1. Understanding school vocabulary words	1	2	3	4	5	6	7
2. Using school vocabulary words when talking	1	2	3	4	5	6	7
3. Figuring out new words when reading	1	2	3	4	5	6	7
4. Spelling words correctly when writing	1	2	3	4	5	6	7
5. Understanding a story when listening	1	2	3	4	5	6	7
6. Telling a story that makes sense	1	2	3	4	5	6	7
7. Understanding a story when reading	1	2	3	4	5	6	7
8. Writing a story that makes sense	1	2	3	4	5	6	7
9. Following spoken directions	1	2	3	4	5	6	7
10. Being organized about schoolwork	1	2	3	4	5	6	7
11. Paying attention in school	1	2	3	4	5	6	7
12. Interacting socially with other students	1	2	3	4	5	6	7

ABILITY CHECKLIST

Please check the things that you think are **easiest** for this student to do:

☐ Art (drawing/painting) ☐ Dance ☐ Music ☐ Mechanical ☐ Sports ☐ Math ☐ Social ☐ Listening ☐ Talking
☐ Reading ☐ Writing ☐ Other: __________

Comments:

Please check the things that you think are **hardest** for this student to do:

☐ Art (drawing/painting) ☐ Dance ☐ Music ☐ Mechanical ☐ Sports ☐ Math ☐ Social ☐ Listening ☐ Talking
☐ Reading ☐ Writing ☐ Other: __________

Comments:

PRIORITY QUESTION

What one thing do you think is most important to help this student do better at school?

Student Language Scale

SLS

TILLS™
TEST OF INTEGRATED LANGUAGE & LITERACY SKILLS™

Nickola Wolf Nelson, Ph.D., CCC-SLP, BCS-CL
Barbara M. Howes, Ph.D., LMSW
Michele A. Anderson, Ph.D., CCC-SLP

This Student Language Scale may be used with the Test of Integrated Language and Literacy Skills™, other assessment tests, or as a stand-alone measure to gather multiple perspectives on a student's language/literacy abilities and other skills.

Student's name: ______________________ Grade: __________ Date: __________

Person responding: ☐ General education teacher ☐ Special education teacher ☐ Other: __________
☐ Student ☐ Parent/guardian

RATING SCALE

Compared with other students of the same age, circle the number to show how good this student is at...	**Not good**						**Very good**
1. Understanding school vocabulary words	1	2	3	4	5	6	7
2. Using school vocabulary words when talking	1	2	3	4	5	6	7
3. Figuring out new words when reading	1	2	3	4	5	6	7
4. Spelling words correctly when writing	1	2	3	4	5	6	7
5. Understanding a story when listening	1	2	3	4	5	6	7
6. Telling a story that makes sense	1	2	3	4	5	6	7
7. Understanding a story when reading	1	2	3	4	5	6	7
8. Writing a story that makes sense	1	2	3	4	5	6	7
9. Following spoken directions	1	2	3	4	5	6	7
10. Being organized about schoolwork	1	2	3	4	5	6	7
11. Paying attention in school	1	2	3	4	5	6	7
12. Interacting socially with other students	1	2	3	4	5	6	7

ABILITY CHECKLIST

Please check the things that you think are **easiest** for this student to do:

☐ Art (drawing/painting) ☐ Dance ☐ Music ☐ Mechanical ☐ Sports ☐ Math ☐ Social ☐ Listening ☐ Talking
☐ Reading ☐ Writing ☐ Other: __________

Comments:

Please check the things that you think are **hardest** for this student to do:

☐ Art (drawing/painting) ☐ Dance ☐ Music ☐ Mechanical ☐ Sports ☐ Math ☐ Social ☐ Listening ☐ Talking
☐ Reading ☐ Writing ☐ Other: __________

Comments:

PRIORITY QUESTION

What one thing do you think is most important to help this student do better at school?

Student Language Scale

SLS

TILLS™
TEST OF INTEGRATED LANGUAGE & LITERACY SKILLS™

Nickola Wolf Nelson, Ph.D., CCC-SLP, BCS-CL
Barbara M. Howes, Ph.D., LMSW
Michele A. Anderson, Ph.D., CCC-SLP

This Student Language Scale may be used with the Test of Integrated Language and Literacy Skills™, other assessment tests, or as a stand-alone measure to gather multiple perspectives on a student's language/literacy abilities and other skills.

Student's name: ______________________ Grade: __________ Date: __________

Person responding: ☐ General education teacher ☐ Special education teacher ☐ Other: __________
☐ Student ☐ Parent/guardian

RATING SCALE

Compared with other students of the same age, circle the number to show how good this student is at...	**Not good**						**Very good**
1. Understanding school vocabulary words	1	2	3	4	5	6	7
2. Using school vocabulary words when talking	1	2	3	4	5	6	7
3. Figuring out new words when reading	1	2	3	4	5	6	7
4. Spelling words correctly when writing	1	2	3	4	5	6	7
5. Understanding a story when listening	1	2	3	4	5	6	7
6. Telling a story that makes sense	1	2	3	4	5	6	7
7. Understanding a story when reading	1	2	3	4	5	6	7
8. Writing a story that makes sense	1	2	3	4	5	6	7
9. Following spoken directions	1	2	3	4	5	6	7
10. Being organized about schoolwork	1	2	3	4	5	6	7
11. Paying attention in school	1	2	3	4	5	6	7
12. Interacting socially with other students	1	2	3	4	5	6	7

ABILITY CHECKLIST

Please check the things that you think are **easiest** for this student to do:

☐ Art (drawing/painting) ☐ Dance ☐ Music ☐ Mechanical ☐ Sports ☐ Math ☐ Social ☐ Listening ☐ Talking
☐ Reading ☐ Writing ☐ Other: __________

Comments:

Please check the things that you think are **hardest** for this student to do:

☐ Art (drawing/painting) ☐ Dance ☐ Music ☐ Mechanical ☐ Sports ☐ Math ☐ Social ☐ Listening ☐ Talking
☐ Reading ☐ Writing ☐ Other: __________

Comments:

PRIORITY QUESTION

What one thing do you think is most important to help this student do better at school?

Student Language Scale

SLS

TILLS™
TEST OF INTEGRATED LANGUAGE & LITERACY SKILLS™

Nickola Wolf Nelson, Ph.D., CCC-SLP, BCS-CL
Barbara M. Howes, Ph.D., LMSW
Michele A. Anderson, Ph.D., CCC-SLP

This Student Language Scale may be used with the Test of Integrated Language and Literacy Skills™, other assessment tests, or as a stand-alone measure to gather multiple perspectives on a student's language/literacy abilities and other skills.

Student's name: ______________________ Grade: __________ Date: __________

Person responding: ☐ General education teacher ☐ Special education teacher ☐ Other: ______________
☐ Student ☐ Parent/guardian

RATING SCALE

Compared with other students of the same age, circle the number to show how good this student is at…	**Not good**						**Very good**
1. Understanding school vocabulary words	1	2	3	4	5	6	7
2. Using school vocabulary words when talking	1	2	3	4	5	6	7
3. Figuring out new words when reading	1	2	3	4	5	6	7
4. Spelling words correctly when writing	1	2	3	4	5	6	7
5. Understanding a story when listening	1	2	3	4	5	6	7
6. Telling a story that makes sense	1	2	3	4	5	6	7
7. Understanding a story when reading	1	2	3	4	5	6	7
8. Writing a story that makes sense	1	2	3	4	5	6	7
9. Following spoken directions	1	2	3	4	5	6	7
10. Being organized about schoolwork	1	2	3	4	5	6	7
11. Paying attention in school	1	2	3	4	5	6	7
12. Interacting socially with other students	1	2	3	4	5	6	7

ABILITY CHECKLIST

Please check the things that you think are **easiest** for this student to do:

☐ Art (drawing/painting) ☐ Dance ☐ Music ☐ Mechanical ☐ Sports ☐ Math ☐ Social ☐ Listening ☐ Talking
☐ Reading ☐ Writing ☐ Other: ______________

Comments:

Please check the things that you think are **hardest** for this student to do:

☐ Art (drawing/painting) ☐ Dance ☐ Music ☐ Mechanical ☐ Sports ☐ Math ☐ Social ☐ Listening ☐ Talking
☐ Reading ☐ Writing ☐ Other: ______________

Comments:

PRIORITY QUESTION

What one thing do you think is most important to help this student do better at school?

P2010301

Student Language Scale

SLS

TILLS™
TEST OF INTEGRATED LANGUAGE & LITERACY SKILLS™

Nickola Wolf Nelson, Ph.D., CCC-SLP, BCS-CL
Barbara M. Howes, Ph.D., LMSW
Michele A. Anderson, Ph.D., CCC-SLP

This Student Language Scale may be used with the Test of Integrated Language and Literacy Skills™, other assessment tests, or as a stand-alone measure to gather multiple perspectives on a student's language/literacy abilities and other skills.

Student's name: ______________________________ Grade: __________ Date: __________

Person responding: ☐ General education teacher ☐ Special education teacher ☐ Other: ______________
☐ Student ☐ Parent/guardian

RATING SCALE

Compared with other students of the same age, circle the number to show how good this student is at...	**Not good**						**Very good**
1. Understanding school vocabulary words	1	2	3	4	5	6	7
2. Using school vocabulary words when talking	1	2	3	4	5	6	7
3. Figuring out new words when reading	1	2	3	4	5	6	7
4. Spelling words correctly when writing	1	2	3	4	5	6	7
5. Understanding a story when listening	1	2	3	4	5	6	7
6. Telling a story that makes sense	1	2	3	4	5	6	7
7. Understanding a story when reading	1	2	3	4	5	6	7
8. Writing a story that makes sense	1	2	3	4	5	6	7
9. Following spoken directions	1	2	3	4	5	6	7
10. Being organized about schoolwork	1	2	3	4	5	6	7
11. Paying attention in school	1	2	3	4	5	6	7
12. Interacting socially with other students	1	2	3	4	5	6	7

ABILITY CHECKLIST

Please check the things that you think are **easiest** for this student to do:

☐ Art (drawing/painting) ☐ Dance ☐ Music ☐ Mechanical ☐ Sports ☐ Math ☐ Social ☐ Listening ☐ Talking
☐ Reading ☐ Writing ☐ Other: ______________

Comments:

Please check the things that you think are **hardest** for this student to do:

☐ Art (drawing/painting) ☐ Dance ☐ Music ☐ Mechanical ☐ Sports ☐ Math ☐ Social ☐ Listening ☐ Talking
☐ Reading ☐ Writing ☐ Other: ______________

Comments:

PRIORITY QUESTION

What one thing do you think is most important to help this student do better at school?

P2010301

Student Language Scale

SLS

TILLS™
TEST OF INTEGRATED LANGUAGE & LITERACY SKILLS™

Nickola Wolf Nelson, Ph.D., CCC-SLP, BCS-CL
Barbara M. Howes, Ph.D., LMSW
Michele A. Anderson, Ph.D., CCC-SLP

This Student Language Scale may be used with the Test of Integrated Language and Literacy Skills™, other assessment tests, or as a stand-alone measure to gather multiple perspectives on a student's language/literacy abilities and other skills.

Student's name: ______________________ Grade: ________ Date: ________

Person responding: ☐ General education teacher ☐ Special education teacher ☐ Other: ______________
☐ Student ☐ Parent/guardian

RATING SCALE

Compared with other students of the same age, circle the number to show how good this student is at...	**Not good**						**Very good**
1. Understanding school vocabulary words	1	2	3	4	5	6	7
2. Using school vocabulary words when talking	1	2	3	4	5	6	7
3. Figuring out new words when reading	1	2	3	4	5	6	7
4. Spelling words correctly when writing	1	2	3	4	5	6	7
5. Understanding a story when listening	1	2	3	4	5	6	7
6. Telling a story that makes sense	1	2	3	4	5	6	7
7. Understanding a story when reading	1	2	3	4	5	6	7
8. Writing a story that makes sense	1	2	3	4	5	6	7
9. Following spoken directions	1	2	3	4	5	6	7
10. Being organized about schoolwork	1	2	3	4	5	6	7
11. Paying attention in school	1	2	3	4	5	6	7
12. Interacting socially with other students	1	2	3	4	5	6	7

ABILITY CHECKLIST

Please check the things that you think are **easiest** for this student to do:

☐ Art (drawing/painting) ☐ Dance ☐ Music ☐ Mechanical ☐ Sports ☐ Math ☐ Social ☐ Listening ☐ Talking
☐ Reading ☐ Writing ☐ Other: ______________

Comments:

Please check the things that you think are **hardest** for this student to do:

☐ Art (drawing/painting) ☐ Dance ☐ Music ☐ Mechanical ☐ Sports ☐ Math ☐ Social ☐ Listening ☐ Talking
☐ Reading ☐ Writing ☐ Other: ______________

Comments:

PRIORITY QUESTION

What one thing do you think is most important to help this student do better at school?

Student Language Scale

SLS

TILLS™
TEST OF INTEGRATED LANGUAGE & LITERACY SKILLS™

Nickola Wolf Nelson, Ph.D., CCC-SLP, BCS-CL
Barbara M. Howes, Ph.D., LMSW
Michele A. Anderson, Ph.D., CCC-SLP

This Student Language Scale may be used with the Test of Integrated Language and Literacy Skills™, other assessment tests, or as a stand-alone measure to gather multiple perspectives on a student's language/literacy abilities and other skills.

Student's name: ______________________ Grade: __________ Date: __________

Person responding: ☐ General education teacher ☐ Special education teacher ☐ Other: __________
☐ Student ☐ Parent/guardian

RATING SCALE

Compared with other students of the same age, circle the number to show how good this student is at...	**Not good**						**Very good**
1. Understanding school vocabulary words	1	2	3	4	5	6	7
2. Using school vocabulary words when talking	1	2	3	4	5	6	7
3. Figuring out new words when reading	1	2	3	4	5	6	7
4. Spelling words correctly when writing	1	2	3	4	5	6	7
5. Understanding a story when listening	1	2	3	4	5	6	7
6. Telling a story that makes sense	1	2	3	4	5	6	7
7. Understanding a story when reading	1	2	3	4	5	6	7
8. Writing a story that makes sense	1	2	3	4	5	6	7
9. Following spoken directions	1	2	3	4	5	6	7
10. Being organized about schoolwork	1	2	3	4	5	6	7
11. Paying attention in school	1	2	3	4	5	6	7
12. Interacting socially with other students	1	2	3	4	5	6	7

ABILITY CHECKLIST

Please check the things that you think are **easiest** for this student to do:

☐ Art (drawing/painting) ☐ Dance ☐ Music ☐ Mechanical ☐ Sports ☐ Math ☐ Social ☐ Listening ☐ Talking
☐ Reading ☐ Writing ☐ Other: __________

Comments:

Please check the things that you think are **hardest** for this student to do:

☐ Art (drawing/painting) ☐ Dance ☐ Music ☐ Mechanical ☐ Sports ☐ Math ☐ Social ☐ Listening ☐ Talking
☐ Reading ☐ Writing ☐ Other: __________

Comments:

PRIORITY QUESTION

What one thing do you think is most important to help this student do better at school?

P2010301

Student Language Scale

SLS

TILLS™ TEST OF INTEGRATED LANGUAGE & LITERACY SKILLS™

Nickola Wolf Nelson, Ph.D., CCC-SLP, BCS-CL
Barbara M. Howes, Ph.D., LMSW
Michele A. Anderson, Ph.D., CCC-SLP

This Student Language Scale may be used with the Test of Integrated Language and Literacy Skills™, other assessment tests, or as a stand-alone measure to gather multiple perspectives on a student's language/literacy abilities and other skills.

Student's name: ______________________ Grade: __________ Date: __________

Person responding: ☐ General education teacher ☐ Special education teacher ☐ Other: __________
☐ Student ☐ Parent/guardian

RATING SCALE

Compared with other students of the same age, circle the number to show how good this student is at...	**Not good**						**Very good**
1. Understanding school vocabulary words	1	2	3	4	5	6	7
2. Using school vocabulary words when talking	1	2	3	4	5	6	7
3. Figuring out new words when reading	1	2	3	4	5	6	7
4. Spelling words correctly when writing	1	2	3	4	5	6	7
5. Understanding a story when listening	1	2	3	4	5	6	7
6. Telling a story that makes sense	1	2	3	4	5	6	7
7. Understanding a story when reading	1	2	3	4	5	6	7
8. Writing a story that makes sense	1	2	3	4	5	6	7
9. Following spoken directions	1	2	3	4	5	6	7
10. Being organized about schoolwork	1	2	3	4	5	6	7
11. Paying attention in school	1	2	3	4	5	6	7
12. Interacting socially with other students	1	2	3	4	5	6	7

ABILITY CHECKLIST

Please check the things that you think are **easiest** for this student to do:

☐ Art (drawing/painting) ☐ Dance ☐ Music ☐ Mechanical ☐ Sports ☐ Math ☐ Social ☐ Listening ☐ Talking
☐ Reading ☐ Writing ☐ Other: __________

Comments:

Please check the things that you think are **hardest** for this student to do:

☐ Art (drawing/painting) ☐ Dance ☐ Music ☐ Mechanical ☐ Sports ☐ Math ☐ Social ☐ Listening ☐ Talking
☐ Reading ☐ Writing ☐ Other: __________

Comments:

PRIORITY QUESTION

What one thing do you think is most important to help this student do better at school?

P2010301

Student Language Scale

TILLS™ TEST OF INTEGRATED LANGUAGE & LITERACY SKILLS™

SLS

Nickola Wolf Nelson, Ph.D., CCC-SLP, BCS-CL
Barbara M. Howes, Ph.D., LMSW
Michele A. Anderson, Ph.D., CCC-SLP

This Student Language Scale may be used with the Test of Integrated Language and Literacy Skills™, other assessment tests, or as a stand-alone measure to gather multiple perspectives on a student's language/literacy abilities and other skills.

Student's name: ______________________ Grade: __________ Date: __________

Person responding: ☐ General education teacher ☐ Special education teacher ☐ Other: __________
☐ Student ☐ Parent/guardian

RATING SCALE

Compared with other students of the same age, circle the number to show how good this student is at...	**Not good**						**Very good**
1. Understanding school vocabulary words	1	2	3	4	5	6	7
2. Using school vocabulary words when talking	1	2	3	4	5	6	7
3. Figuring out new words when reading	1	2	3	4	5	6	7
4. Spelling words correctly when writing	1	2	3	4	5	6	7
5. Understanding a story when listening	1	2	3	4	5	6	7
6. Telling a story that makes sense	1	2	3	4	5	6	7
7. Understanding a story when reading	1	2	3	4	5	6	7
8. Writing a story that makes sense	1	2	3	4	5	6	7
9. Following spoken directions	1	2	3	4	5	6	7
10. Being organized about schoolwork	1	2	3	4	5	6	7
11. Paying attention in school	1	2	3	4	5	6	7
12. Interacting socially with other students	1	2	3	4	5	6	7

ABILITY CHECKLIST

Please check the things that you think are **easiest** for this student to do:

☐ Art (drawing/painting) ☐ Dance ☐ Music ☐ Mechanical ☐ Sports ☐ Math ☐ Social ☐ Listening ☐ Talking
☐ Reading ☐ Writing ☐ Other: __________

Comments:

Please check the things that you think are **hardest** for this student to do:

☐ Art (drawing/painting) ☐ Dance ☐ Music ☐ Mechanical ☐ Sports ☐ Math ☐ Social ☐ Listening ☐ Talking
☐ Reading ☐ Writing ☐ Other: __________

Comments:

PRIORITY QUESTION

What one thing do you think is most important to help this student do better at school?

Student Language Scale

SLS

TILLS™
TEST OF INTEGRATED LANGUAGE & LITERACY SKILLS™

Nickola Wolf Nelson, Ph.D., CCC-SLP, BCS-CL
Barbara M. Howes, Ph.D., LMSW
Michele A. Anderson, Ph.D., CCC-SLP

This Student Language Scale may be used with the Test of Integrated Language and Literacy Skills™, other assessment tests, or as a stand-alone measure to gather multiple perspectives on a student's language/literacy abilities and other skills.

Student's name: ______________________ Grade: __________ Date: __________

Person responding: ☐ General education teacher ☐ Special education teacher ☐ Other: ______________
☐ Student ☐ Parent/guardian

RATING SCALE

Compared with other students of the same age, circle the number to show how good this student is at...	**Not good**						**Very good**
1. Understanding school vocabulary words	1	2	3	4	5	6	7
2. Using school vocabulary words when talking	1	2	3	4	5	6	7
3. Figuring out new words when reading	1	2	3	4	5	6	7
4. Spelling words correctly when writing	1	2	3	4	5	6	7
5. Understanding a story when listening	1	2	3	4	5	6	7
6. Telling a story that makes sense	1	2	3	4	5	6	7
7. Understanding a story when reading	1	2	3	4	5	6	7
8. Writing a story that makes sense	1	2	3	4	5	6	7
9. Following spoken directions	1	2	3	4	5	6	7
10. Being organized about schoolwork	1	2	3	4	5	6	7
11. Paying attention in school	1	2	3	4	5	6	7
12. Interacting socially with other students	1	2	3	4	5	6	7

ABILITY CHECKLIST

Please check the things that you think are **easiest** for this student to do:

☐ Art (drawing/painting) ☐ Dance ☐ Music ☐ Mechanical ☐ Sports ☐ Math ☐ Social ☐ Listening ☐ Talking
☐ Reading ☐ Writing ☐ Other: ______________

Comments:

Please check the things that you think are **hardest** for this student to do:

☐ Art (drawing/painting) ☐ Dance ☐ Music ☐ Mechanical ☐ Sports ☐ Math ☐ Social ☐ Listening ☐ Talking
☐ Reading ☐ Writing ☐ Other: ______________

Comments:

PRIORITY QUESTION

What one thing do you think is most important to help this student do better at school?

P2010301

Student Language Scale

SLS

TILLS™
TEST OF INTEGRATED LANGUAGE & LITERACY SKILLS™

Nickola Wolf Nelson, Ph.D., CCC-SLP, BCS-CL
Barbara M. Howes, Ph.D., LMSW
Michele A. Anderson, Ph.D., CCC-SLP

This Student Language Scale may be used with the Test of Integrated Language and Literacy Skills™, other assessment tests, or as a stand-alone measure to gather multiple perspectives on a student's language/literacy abilities and other skills.

Student's name: ______________________________ Grade: __________ Date: __________

Person responding: ☐ General education teacher ☐ Special education teacher ☐ Other: ______________
☐ Student ☐ Parent/guardian

RATING SCALE

Compared with other students of the same age, circle the number to show how good this student is at...	**Not good**						**Very good**
1. Understanding school vocabulary words	1	2	3	4	5	6	7
2. Using school vocabulary words when talking	1	2	3	4	5	6	7
3. Figuring out new words when reading	1	2	3	4	5	6	7
4. Spelling words correctly when writing	1	2	3	4	5	6	7
5. Understanding a story when listening	1	2	3	4	5	6	7
6. Telling a story that makes sense	1	2	3	4	5	6	7
7. Understanding a story when reading	1	2	3	4	5	6	7
8. Writing a story that makes sense	1	2	3	4	5	6	7
9. Following spoken directions	1	2	3	4	5	6	7
10. Being organized about schoolwork	1	2	3	4	5	6	7
11. Paying attention in school	1	2	3	4	5	6	7
12. Interacting socially with other students	1	2	3	4	5	6	7

ABILITY CHECKLIST

Please check the things that you think are **easiest** for this student to do:

☐ Art (drawing/painting) ☐ Dance ☐ Music ☐ Mechanical ☐ Sports ☐ Math ☐ Social ☐ Listening ☐ Talking
☐ Reading ☐ Writing ☐ Other: ______________

Comments:

Please check the things that you think are **hardest** for this student to do:

☐ Art (drawing/painting) ☐ Dance ☐ Music ☐ Mechanical ☐ Sports ☐ Math ☐ Social ☐ Listening ☐ Talking
☐ Reading ☐ Writing ☐ Other: ______________

Comments:

PRIORITY QUESTION

What one thing do you think is most important to help this student do better at school?

P2010301

Student Language Scale

SLS

TILLS™ TEST OF INTEGRATED LANGUAGE & LITERACY SKILLS™

Nickola Wolf Nelson, Ph.D., CCC-SLP, BCS-CL
Barbara M. Howes, Ph.D., LMSW
Michele A. Anderson, Ph.D., CCC-SLP

This Student Language Scale may be used with the Test of Integrated Language and Literacy Skills™, other assessment tests, or as a stand-alone measure to gather multiple perspectives on a student's language/literacy abilities and other skills.

Student's name: ______________________________ Grade: __________ Date: __________

Person responding: ☐ General education teacher ☐ Special education teacher ☐ Other: ____________
☐ Student ☐ Parent/guardian

RATING SCALE

Compared with other students of the same age, circle the number to show how good this student is at...	**Not good**						**Very good**
1. Understanding school vocabulary words	1	2	3	4	5	6	7
2. Using school vocabulary words when talking	1	2	3	4	5	6	7
3. Figuring out new words when reading	1	2	3	4	5	6	7
4. Spelling words correctly when writing	1	2	3	4	5	6	7
5. Understanding a story when listening	1	2	3	4	5	6	7
6. Telling a story that makes sense	1	2	3	4	5	6	7
7. Understanding a story when reading	1	2	3	4	5	6	7
8. Writing a story that makes sense	1	2	3	4	5	6	7
9. Following spoken directions	1	2	3	4	5	6	7
10. Being organized about schoolwork	1	2	3	4	5	6	7
11. Paying attention in school	1	2	3	4	5	6	7
12. Interacting socially with other students	1	2	3	4	5	6	7

ABILITY CHECKLIST

Please check the things that you think are **easiest** for this student to do:

☐ Art (drawing/painting) ☐ Dance ☐ Music ☐ Mechanical ☐ Sports ☐ Math ☐ Social ☐ Listening ☐ Talking
☐ Reading ☐ Writing ☐ Other: ______________

Comments:

Please check the things that you think are **hardest** for this student to do:

☐ Art (drawing/painting) ☐ Dance ☐ Music ☐ Mechanical ☐ Sports ☐ Math ☐ Social ☐ Listening ☐ Talking
☐ Reading ☐ Writing ☐ Other: ______________

Comments:

PRIORITY QUESTION

What one thing do you think is most important to help this student do better at school?

Student Language Scale

SLS

TILLS™
TEST OF INTEGRATED LANGUAGE & LITERACY SKILLS™

Nickola Wolf Nelson, Ph.D., CCC-SLP, BCS-CL
Barbara M. Howes, Ph.D., LMSW
Michele A. Anderson, Ph.D., CCC-SLP

This Student Language Scale may be used with the Test of Integrated Language and Literacy Skills™, other assessment tests, or as a stand-alone measure to gather multiple perspectives on a student's language/literacy abilities and other skills.

Student's name: ______________________________ Grade: __________ Date: __________

Person responding: ☐ General education teacher ☐ Special education teacher ☐ Other: ______________
☐ Student ☐ Parent/guardian

RATING SCALE

Compared with other students of the same age, circle the number to show how good this student is at...	**Not good**						**Very good**
1. Understanding school vocabulary words	1	2	3	4	5	6	7
2. Using school vocabulary words when talking	1	2	3	4	5	6	7
3. Figuring out new words when reading	1	2	3	4	5	6	7
4. Spelling words correctly when writing	1	2	3	4	5	6	7
5. Understanding a story when listening	1	2	3	4	5	6	7
6. Telling a story that makes sense	1	2	3	4	5	6	7
7. Understanding a story when reading	1	2	3	4	5	6	7
8. Writing a story that makes sense	1	2	3	4	5	6	7
9. Following spoken directions	1	2	3	4	5	6	7
10. Being organized about schoolwork	1	2	3	4	5	6	7
11. Paying attention in school	1	2	3	4	5	6	7
12. Interacting socially with other students	1	2	3	4	5	6	7

ABILITY CHECKLIST

Please check the things that you think are **easiest** for this student to do:

☐ Art (drawing/painting) ☐ Dance ☐ Music ☐ Mechanical ☐ Sports ☐ Math ☐ Social ☐ Listening ☐ Talking
☐ Reading ☐ Writing ☐ Other: ______________

Comments:

Please check the things that you think are **hardest** for this student to do:

☐ Art (drawing/painting) ☐ Dance ☐ Music ☐ Mechanical ☐ Sports ☐ Math ☐ Social ☐ Listening ☐ Talking
☐ Reading ☐ Writing ☐ Other: ______________

Comments:

PRIORITY QUESTION

What one thing do you think is most important to help this student do better at school?

Student Language Scale

SLS

TILLS™
TEST OF INTEGRATED LANGUAGE & LITERACY SKILLS™

Nickola Wolf Nelson, Ph.D., CCC-SLP, BCS-CL
Barbara M. Howes, Ph.D., LMSW
Michele A. Anderson, Ph.D., CCC-SLP

This Student Language Scale may be used with the Test of Integrated Language and Literacy Skills™, other assessment tests, or as a stand-alone measure to gather multiple perspectives on a student's language/literacy abilities and other skills.

Student's name: ______________________ Grade: __________ Date: __________

Person responding: ☐ General education teacher ☐ Special education teacher ☐ Other: ______________
☐ Student ☐ Parent/guardian

RATING SCALE

Compared with other students of the same age, circle the number to show how good this student is at...	**Not good**						**Very good**
1. Understanding school vocabulary words	1	2	3	4	5	6	7
2. Using school vocabulary words when talking	1	2	3	4	5	6	7
3. Figuring out new words when reading	1	2	3	4	5	6	7
4. Spelling words correctly when writing	1	2	3	4	5	6	7
5. Understanding a story when listening	1	2	3	4	5	6	7
6. Telling a story that makes sense	1	2	3	4	5	6	7
7. Understanding a story when reading	1	2	3	4	5	6	7
8. Writing a story that makes sense	1	2	3	4	5	6	7
9. Following spoken directions	1	2	3	4	5	6	7
10. Being organized about schoolwork	1	2	3	4	5	6	7
11. Paying attention in school	1	2	3	4	5	6	7
12. Interacting socially with other students	1	2	3	4	5	6	7

ABILITY CHECKLIST

Please check the things that you think are **easiest** for this student to do:

☐ Art (drawing/painting) ☐ Dance ☐ Music ☐ Mechanical ☐ Sports ☐ Math ☐ Social ☐ Listening ☐ Talking
☐ Reading ☐ Writing ☐ Other: ______________

Comments:

Please check the things that you think are **hardest** for this student to do:

☐ Art (drawing/painting) ☐ Dance ☐ Music ☐ Mechanical ☐ Sports ☐ Math ☐ Social ☐ Listening ☐ Talking
☐ Reading ☐ Writing ☐ Other: ______________

Comments:

PRIORITY QUESTION

What one thing do you think is most important to help this student do better at school?

Student Language Scale

SLS

TILLS™
TEST OF INTEGRATED LANGUAGE & LITERACY SKILLS™

Nickola Wolf Nelson, Ph.D., CCC-SLP, BCS-CL
Barbara M. Howes, Ph.D., LMSW
Michele A. Anderson, Ph.D., CCC-SLP

This Student Language Scale may be used with the Test of Integrated Language and Literacy Skills™, other assessment tests, or as a stand-alone measure to gather multiple perspectives on a student's language/literacy abilities and other skills.

Student's name: ______________________ Grade: __________ Date: __________

Person responding: ☐ General education teacher ☐ Special education teacher ☐ Other: __________
☐ Student ☐ Parent/guardian

RATING SCALE

Compared with other students of the same age, circle the number to show how good this student is at...	**Not good**						**Very good**
1. Understanding school vocabulary words	1	2	3	4	5	6	7
2. Using school vocabulary words when talking	1	2	3	4	5	6	7
3. Figuring out new words when reading	1	2	3	4	5	6	7
4. Spelling words correctly when writing	1	2	3	4	5	6	7
5. Understanding a story when listening	1	2	3	4	5	6	7
6. Telling a story that makes sense	1	2	3	4	5	6	7
7. Understanding a story when reading	1	2	3	4	5	6	7
8. Writing a story that makes sense	1	2	3	4	5	6	7
9. Following spoken directions	1	2	3	4	5	6	7
10. Being organized about schoolwork	1	2	3	4	5	6	7
11. Paying attention in school	1	2	3	4	5	6	7
12. Interacting socially with other students	1	2	3	4	5	6	7

ABILITY CHECKLIST

Please check the things that you think are **easiest** for this student to do:

☐ Art (drawing/painting) ☐ Dance ☐ Music ☐ Mechanical ☐ Sports ☐ Math ☐ Social ☐ Listening ☐ Talking
☐ Reading ☐ Writing ☐ Other: __________

Comments:

Please check the things that you think are **hardest** for this student to do:

☐ Art (drawing/painting) ☐ Dance ☐ Music ☐ Mechanical ☐ Sports ☐ Math ☐ Social ☐ Listening ☐ Talking
☐ Reading ☐ Writing ☐ Other: __________

Comments:

PRIORITY QUESTION

What one thing do you think is most important to help this student do better at school?

P2010301

Student Language Scale

SLS

TILLS™ TEST OF INTEGRATED LANGUAGE & LITERACY SKILLS™

Nickola Wolf Nelson, Ph.D., CCC-SLP, BCS-CL
Barbara M. Howes, Ph.D., LMSW
Michele A. Anderson, Ph.D., CCC-SLP

This Student Language Scale may be used with the Test of Integrated Language and Literacy Skills™, other assessment tests, or as a stand-alone measure to gather multiple perspectives on a student's language/literacy abilities and other skills.

Student's name: ______________________ Grade: ________ Date: ________

Person responding: ☐ General education teacher ☐ Special education teacher ☐ Other: ____________
☐ Student ☐ Parent/guardian

RATING SCALE

Compared with other students of the same age, circle the number to show how good this student is at...	**Not good**						**Very good**
1. Understanding school vocabulary words	1	2	3	4	5	6	7
2. Using school vocabulary words when talking	1	2	3	4	5	6	7
3. Figuring out new words when reading	1	2	3	4	5	6	7
4. Spelling words correctly when writing	1	2	3	4	5	6	7
5. Understanding a story when listening	1	2	3	4	5	6	7
6. Telling a story that makes sense	1	2	3	4	5	6	7
7. Understanding a story when reading	1	2	3	4	5	6	7
8. Writing a story that makes sense	1	2	3	4	5	6	7
9. Following spoken directions	1	2	3	4	5	6	7
10. Being organized about schoolwork	1	2	3	4	5	6	7
11. Paying attention in school	1	2	3	4	5	6	7
12. Interacting socially with other students	1	2	3	4	5	6	7

ABILITY CHECKLIST

Please check the things that you think are **easiest** for this student to do:

☐ Art (drawing/painting) ☐ Dance ☐ Music ☐ Mechanical ☐ Sports ☐ Math ☐ Social ☐ Listening ☐ Talking
☐ Reading ☐ Writing ☐ Other: ____________

Comments:

Please check the things that you think are **hardest** for this student to do:

☐ Art (drawing/painting) ☐ Dance ☐ Music ☐ Mechanical ☐ Sports ☐ Math ☐ Social ☐ Listening ☐ Talking
☐ Reading ☐ Writing ☐ Other: ____________

Comments:

PRIORITY QUESTION

What one thing do you think is most important to help this student do better at school?

P2010301

Student Language Scale

SLS

TILLS™
TEST OF INTEGRATED LANGUAGE & LITERACY SKILLS™

Nickola Wolf Nelson, Ph.D., CCC-SLP, BCS-CL
Barbara M. Howes, Ph.D., LMSW
Michele A. Anderson, Ph.D., CCC-SLP

This Student Language Scale may be used with the Test of Integrated Language and Literacy Skills™, other assessment tests, or as a stand-alone measure to gather multiple perspectives on a student's language/literacy abilities and other skills.

Student's name: ______________________ Grade: ________ Date: ________

Person responding: ☐ General education teacher ☐ Special education teacher ☐ Other: ____________
☐ Student ☐ Parent/guardian

RATING SCALE

Compared with other students of the same age, circle the number to show how good this student is at...	**Not good**						**Very good**
1. Understanding school vocabulary words	1	2	3	4	5	6	7
2. Using school vocabulary words when talking	1	2	3	4	5	6	7
3. Figuring out new words when reading	1	2	3	4	5	6	7
4. Spelling words correctly when writing	1	2	3	4	5	6	7
5. Understanding a story when listening	1	2	3	4	5	6	7
6. Telling a story that makes sense	1	2	3	4	5	6	7
7. Understanding a story when reading	1	2	3	4	5	6	7
8. Writing a story that makes sense	1	2	3	4	5	6	7
9. Following spoken directions	1	2	3	4	5	6	7
10. Being organized about schoolwork	1	2	3	4	5	6	7
11. Paying attention in school	1	2	3	4	5	6	7
12. Interacting socially with other students	1	2	3	4	5	6	7

ABILITY CHECKLIST

Please check the things that you think are **easiest** for this student to do:

☐ Art (drawing/painting) ☐ Dance ☐ Music ☐ Mechanical ☐ Sports ☐ Math ☐ Social ☐ Listening ☐ Talking
☐ Reading ☐ Writing ☐ Other: ____________

Comments:

Please check the things that you think are **hardest** for this student to do:

☐ Art (drawing/painting) ☐ Dance ☐ Music ☐ Mechanical ☐ Sports ☐ Math ☐ Social ☐ Listening ☐ Talking
☐ Reading ☐ Writing ☐ Other: ____________

Comments:

PRIORITY QUESTION

What one thing do you think is most important to help this student do better at school?

P2010301

Student Language Scale

SLS

TILLS™
TEST OF INTEGRATED LANGUAGE & LITERACY SKILLS™

Nickola Wolf Nelson, Ph.D., CCC-SLP, BCS-CL
Barbara M. Howes, Ph.D., LMSW
Michele A. Anderson, Ph.D., CCC-SLP

This Student Language Scale may be used with the Test of Integrated Language and Literacy Skills™, other assessment tests, or as a stand-alone measure to gather multiple perspectives on a student's language/literacy abilities and other skills.

Student's name: ______________________ Grade: ________ Date: ________

Person responding: ☐ General education teacher ☐ Special education teacher ☐ Other: ____________
☐ Student ☐ Parent/guardian

RATING SCALE

Compared with other students of the same age, circle the number to show how good this student is at...	**Not good**						**Very good**
1. Understanding school vocabulary words	1	2	3	4	5	6	7
2. Using school vocabulary words when talking	1	2	3	4	5	6	7
3. Figuring out new words when reading	1	2	3	4	5	6	7
4. Spelling words correctly when writing	1	2	3	4	5	6	7
5. Understanding a story when listening	1	2	3	4	5	6	7
6. Telling a story that makes sense	1	2	3	4	5	6	7
7. Understanding a story when reading	1	2	3	4	5	6	7
8. Writing a story that makes sense	1	2	3	4	5	6	7
9. Following spoken directions	1	2	3	4	5	6	7
10. Being organized about schoolwork	1	2	3	4	5	6	7
11. Paying attention in school	1	2	3	4	5	6	7
12. Interacting socially with other students	1	2	3	4	5	6	7

ABILITY CHECKLIST

Please check the things that you think are **easiest** for this student to do:

☐ Art (drawing/painting) ☐ Dance ☐ Music ☐ Mechanical ☐ Sports ☐ Math ☐ Social ☐ Listening ☐ Talking
☐ Reading ☐ Writing ☐ Other: ____________

Comments:

Please check the things that you think are **hardest** for this student to do:

☐ Art (drawing/painting) ☐ Dance ☐ Music ☐ Mechanical ☐ Sports ☐ Math ☐ Social ☐ Listening ☐ Talking
☐ Reading ☐ Writing ☐ Other: ____________

Comments:

PRIORITY QUESTION

What one thing do you think is most important to help this student do better at school?

Student Language Scale

SLS

TILLS™
TEST OF INTEGRATED LANGUAGE & LITERACY SKILLS™

Nickola Wolf Nelson, Ph.D., CCC-SLP, BCS-CL
Barbara M. Howes, Ph.D., LMSW
Michele A. Anderson, Ph.D., CCC-SLP

This Student Language Scale may be used with the Test of Integrated Language and Literacy Skills™, other assessment tests, or as a stand-alone measure to gather multiple perspectives on a student's language/literacy abilities and other skills.

Student's name: ______________________ Grade: __________ Date: __________

Person responding: ☐ General education teacher ☐ Special education teacher ☐ Other: __________
☐ Student ☐ Parent/guardian

RATING SCALE

Compared with other students of the same age, circle the number to show how good this student is at...	**Not good**						**Very good**
1. Understanding school vocabulary words	1	2	3	4	5	6	7
2. Using school vocabulary words when talking	1	2	3	4	5	6	7
3. Figuring out new words when reading	1	2	3	4	5	6	7
4. Spelling words correctly when writing	1	2	3	4	5	6	7
5. Understanding a story when listening	1	2	3	4	5	6	7
6. Telling a story that makes sense	1	2	3	4	5	6	7
7. Understanding a story when reading	1	2	3	4	5	6	7
8. Writing a story that makes sense	1	2	3	4	5	6	7
9. Following spoken directions	1	2	3	4	5	6	7
10. Being organized about schoolwork	1	2	3	4	5	6	7
11. Paying attention in school	1	2	3	4	5	6	7
12. Interacting socially with other students	1	2	3	4	5	6	7

ABILITY CHECKLIST

Please check the things that you think are **easiest** for this student to do:

☐ Art (drawing/painting) ☐ Dance ☐ Music ☐ Mechanical ☐ Sports ☐ Math ☐ Social ☐ Listening ☐ Talking
☐ Reading ☐ Writing ☐ Other: __________

Comments:

Please check the things that you think are **hardest** for this student to do:

☐ Art (drawing/painting) ☐ Dance ☐ Music ☐ Mechanical ☐ Sports ☐ Math ☐ Social ☐ Listening ☐ Talking
☐ Reading ☐ Writing ☐ Other: __________

Comments:

PRIORITY QUESTION

What one thing do you think is most important to help this student do better at school?

Student Language Scale

SLS

TILLS™
TEST OF INTEGRATED LANGUAGE & LITERACY SKILLS™

Nickola Wolf Nelson, Ph.D., CCC-SLP, BCS-CL
Barbara M. Howes, Ph.D., LMSW
Michele A. Anderson, Ph.D., CCC-SLP

This Student Language Scale may be used with the Test of Integrated Language and Literacy Skills™, other assessment tests, or as a stand-alone measure to gather multiple perspectives on a student's language/literacy abilities and other skills.

Student's name: ______________________ Grade: ________ Date: ________

Person responding: ☐ General education teacher ☐ Special education teacher ☐ Other: ______________
☐ Student ☐ Parent/guardian

RATING SCALE

Compared with other students of the same age, circle the number to show how good this student is at...	**Not good**						**Very good**
1. Understanding school vocabulary words	1	2	3	4	5	6	7
2. Using school vocabulary words when talking	1	2	3	4	5	6	7
3. Figuring out new words when reading	1	2	3	4	5	6	7
4. Spelling words correctly when writing	1	2	3	4	5	6	7
5. Understanding a story when listening	1	2	3	4	5	6	7
6. Telling a story that makes sense	1	2	3	4	5	6	7
7. Understanding a story when reading	1	2	3	4	5	6	7
8. Writing a story that makes sense	1	2	3	4	5	6	7
9. Following spoken directions	1	2	3	4	5	6	7
10. Being organized about schoolwork	1	2	3	4	5	6	7
11. Paying attention in school	1	2	3	4	5	6	7
12. Interacting socially with other students	1	2	3	4	5	6	7

ABILITY CHECKLIST

Please check the things that you think are **easiest** for this student to do:

☐ Art (drawing/painting) ☐ Dance ☐ Music ☐ Mechanical ☐ Sports ☐ Math ☐ Social ☐ Listening ☐ Talking
☐ Reading ☐ Writing ☐ Other: ______________

Comments:

Please check the things that you think are **hardest** for this student to do:

☐ Art (drawing/painting) ☐ Dance ☐ Music ☐ Mechanical ☐ Sports ☐ Math ☐ Social ☐ Listening ☐ Talking
☐ Reading ☐ Writing ☐ Other: ______________

Comments:

PRIORITY QUESTION

What one thing do you think is most important to help this student do better at school?

P2010301

Student Language Scale

SLS

TILLS™
TEST OF INTEGRATED LANGUAGE & LITERACY SKILLS™

Nickola Wolf Nelson, Ph.D., CCC-SLP, BCS-CL
Barbara M. Howes, Ph.D., LMSW
Michele A. Anderson, Ph.D., CCC-SLP

This Student Language Scale may be used with the Test of Integrated Language and Literacy Skills™, other assessment tests, or as a stand-alone measure to gather multiple perspectives on a student's language/literacy abilities and other skills.

Student's name: ______________________________ Grade: __________ Date: __________

Person responding: ☐ General education teacher ☐ Special education teacher ☐ Other: __________
☐ Student ☐ Parent/guardian

RATING SCALE

Compared with other students of the same age, circle the number to show how good this student is at...	**Not good**						**Very good**
1. Understanding school vocabulary words	1	2	3	4	5	6	7
2. Using school vocabulary words when talking	1	2	3	4	5	6	7
3. Figuring out new words when reading	1	2	3	4	5	6	7
4. Spelling words correctly when writing	1	2	3	4	5	6	7
5. Understanding a story when listening	1	2	3	4	5	6	7
6. Telling a story that makes sense	1	2	3	4	5	6	7
7. Understanding a story when reading	1	2	3	4	5	6	7
8. Writing a story that makes sense	1	2	3	4	5	6	7
9. Following spoken directions	1	2	3	4	5	6	7
10. Being organized about schoolwork	1	2	3	4	5	6	7
11. Paying attention in school	1	2	3	4	5	6	7
12. Interacting socially with other students	1	2	3	4	5	6	7

ABILITY CHECKLIST

Please check the things that you think are **easiest** for this student to do:

☐ Art (drawing/painting) ☐ Dance ☐ Music ☐ Mechanical ☐ Sports ☐ Math ☐ Social ☐ Listening ☐ Talking
☐ Reading ☐ Writing ☐ Other: __________

Comments:

Please check the things that you think are **hardest** for this student to do:

☐ Art (drawing/painting) ☐ Dance ☐ Music ☐ Mechanical ☐ Sports ☐ Math ☐ Social ☐ Listening ☐ Talking
☐ Reading ☐ Writing ☐ Other: __________

Comments:

PRIORITY QUESTION

What one thing do you think is most important to help this student do better at school?

Student Language Scale

SLS

TILLS™
TEST OF INTEGRATED LANGUAGE & LITERACY SKILLS™

Nickola Wolf Nelson, Ph.D., CCC-SLP, BCS-CL
Barbara M. Howes, Ph.D., LMSW
Michele A. Anderson, Ph.D., CCC-SLP

This Student Language Scale may be used with the Test of Integrated Language and Literacy Skills™, other assessment tests, or as a stand-alone measure to gather multiple perspectives on a student's language/literacy abilities and other skills.

Student's name: ______________________________ Grade: __________ Date: __________

Person responding: ☐ General education teacher ☐ Special education teacher ☐ Other: __________
☐ Student ☐ Parent/guardian

RATING SCALE

Compared with other students of the same age, circle the number to show how good this student is at...	**Not good**						**Very good**
1. Understanding school vocabulary words	1	2	3	4	5	6	7
2. Using school vocabulary words when talking	1	2	3	4	5	6	7
3. Figuring out new words when reading	1	2	3	4	5	6	7
4. Spelling words correctly when writing	1	2	3	4	5	6	7
5. Understanding a story when listening	1	2	3	4	5	6	7
6. Telling a story that makes sense	1	2	3	4	5	6	7
7. Understanding a story when reading	1	2	3	4	5	6	7
8. Writing a story that makes sense	1	2	3	4	5	6	7
9. Following spoken directions	1	2	3	4	5	6	7
10. Being organized about schoolwork	1	2	3	4	5	6	7
11. Paying attention in school	1	2	3	4	5	6	7
12. Interacting socially with other students	1	2	3	4	5	6	7

ABILITY CHECKLIST

Please check the things that you think are **easiest** for this student to do:

☐ Art (drawing/painting) ☐ Dance ☐ Music ☐ Mechanical ☐ Sports ☐ Math ☐ Social ☐ Listening ☐ Talking
☐ Reading ☐ Writing ☐ Other: __________

Comments:

Please check the things that you think are **hardest** for this student to do:

☐ Art (drawing/painting) ☐ Dance ☐ Music ☐ Mechanical ☐ Sports ☐ Math ☐ Social ☐ Listening ☐ Talking
☐ Reading ☐ Writing ☐ Other: __________

Comments:

PRIORITY QUESTION

What one thing do you think is most important to help this student do better at school?

P2010301

Student Language Scale

SLS

TILLS™
TEST OF INTEGRATED LANGUAGE & LITERACY SKILLS™

Nickola Wolf Nelson, Ph.D., CCC-SLP, BCS-CL
Barbara M. Howes, Ph.D., LMSW
Michele A. Anderson, Ph.D., CCC-SLP

This Student Language Scale may be used with the Test of Integrated Language and Literacy Skills™, other assessment tests, or as a stand-alone measure to gather multiple perspectives on a student's language/literacy abilities and other skills.

Student's name: ______________________ Grade: __________ Date: __________

Person responding: ☐ General education teacher ☐ Special education teacher ☐ Other: __________
☐ Student ☐ Parent/guardian

RATING SCALE

Compared with other students of the same age, circle the number to show how good this student is at...	**Not good**						**Very good**
1. Understanding school vocabulary words	1	2	3	4	5	6	7
2. Using school vocabulary words when talking	1	2	3	4	5	6	7
3. Figuring out new words when reading	1	2	3	4	5	6	7
4. Spelling words correctly when writing	1	2	3	4	5	6	7
5. Understanding a story when listening	1	2	3	4	5	6	7
6. Telling a story that makes sense	1	2	3	4	5	6	7
7. Understanding a story when reading	1	2	3	4	5	6	7
8. Writing a story that makes sense	1	2	3	4	5	6	7
9. Following spoken directions	1	2	3	4	5	6	7
10. Being organized about schoolwork	1	2	3	4	5	6	7
11. Paying attention in school	1	2	3	4	5	6	7
12. Interacting socially with other students	1	2	3	4	5	6	7

ABILITY CHECKLIST

Please check the things that you think are **easiest** for this student to do:

☐ Art (drawing/painting) ☐ Dance ☐ Music ☐ Mechanical ☐ Sports ☐ Math ☐ Social ☐ Listening ☐ Talking
☐ Reading ☐ Writing ☐ Other: __________

Comments:

Please check the things that you think are **hardest** for this student to do:

☐ Art (drawing/painting) ☐ Dance ☐ Music ☐ Mechanical ☐ Sports ☐ Math ☐ Social ☐ Listening ☐ Talking
☐ Reading ☐ Writing ☐ Other: __________

Comments:

PRIORITY QUESTION

What one thing do you think is most important to help this student do better at school?

P2010301

Student Language Scale

SLS

TILLS™
TEST OF INTEGRATED LANGUAGE & LITERACY SKILLS™

Nickola Wolf Nelson, Ph.D., CCC-SLP, BCS-CL
Barbara M. Howes, Ph.D., LMSW
Michele A. Anderson, Ph.D., CCC-SLP

This Student Language Scale may be used with the Test of Integrated Language and Literacy Skills™, other assessment tests, or as a stand-alone measure to gather multiple perspectives on a student's language/literacy abilities and other skills.

Student's name: ______________________ Grade: __________ Date: __________

Person responding: ☐ General education teacher ☐ Special education teacher ☐ Other: __________
☐ Student ☐ Parent/guardian

RATING SCALE

Compared with other students of the same age, circle the number to show how good this student is at...	**Not good**						**Very good**
1. Understanding school vocabulary words	1	2	3	4	5	6	7
2. Using school vocabulary words when talking	1	2	3	4	5	6	7
3. Figuring out new words when reading	1	2	3	4	5	6	7
4. Spelling words correctly when writing	1	2	3	4	5	6	7
5. Understanding a story when listening	1	2	3	4	5	6	7
6. Telling a story that makes sense	1	2	3	4	5	6	7
7. Understanding a story when reading	1	2	3	4	5	6	7
8. Writing a story that makes sense	1	2	3	4	5	6	7
9. Following spoken directions	1	2	3	4	5	6	7
10. Being organized about schoolwork	1	2	3	4	5	6	7
11. Paying attention in school	1	2	3	4	5	6	7
12. Interacting socially with other students	1	2	3	4	5	6	7

ABILITY CHECKLIST

Please check the things that you think are **easiest** for this student to do:

☐ Art (drawing/painting) ☐ Dance ☐ Music ☐ Mechanical ☐ Sports ☐ Math ☐ Social ☐ Listening ☐ Talking
☐ Reading ☐ Writing ☐ Other: __________

Comments:

Please check the things that you think are **hardest** for this student to do:

☐ Art (drawing/painting) ☐ Dance ☐ Music ☐ Mechanical ☐ Sports ☐ Math ☐ Social ☐ Listening ☐ Talking
☐ Reading ☐ Writing ☐ Other: __________

Comments:

PRIORITY QUESTION

What one thing do you think is most important to help this student do better at school?

P2010301

Student Language Scale

SLS

TILLS™
TEST OF INTEGRATED LANGUAGE & LITERACY SKILLS™

Nickola Wolf Nelson, Ph.D., CCC-SLP, BCS-CL
Barbara M. Howes, Ph.D., LMSW
Michele A. Anderson, Ph.D., CCC-SLP

This Student Language Scale may be used with the Test of Integrated Language and Literacy Skills™, other assessment tests, or as a stand-alone measure to gather multiple perspectives on a student's language/literacy abilities and other skills.

Student's name: ______________________________ Grade: __________ Date: __________

Person responding: ☐ General education teacher ☐ Special education teacher ☐ Other: ______________
☐ Student ☐ Parent/guardian

RATING SCALE

Compared with other students of the same age, circle the number to show how good this student is at...	**Not good**						**Very good**
1. Understanding school vocabulary words	1	2	3	4	5	6	7
2. Using school vocabulary words when talking	1	2	3	4	5	6	7
3. Figuring out new words when reading	1	2	3	4	5	6	7
4. Spelling words correctly when writing	1	2	3	4	5	6	7
5. Understanding a story when listening	1	2	3	4	5	6	7
6. Telling a story that makes sense	1	2	3	4	5	6	7
7. Understanding a story when reading	1	2	3	4	5	6	7
8. Writing a story that makes sense	1	2	3	4	5	6	7
9. Following spoken directions	1	2	3	4	5	6	7
10. Being organized about schoolwork	1	2	3	4	5	6	7
11. Paying attention in school	1	2	3	4	5	6	7
12. Interacting socially with other students	1	2	3	4	5	6	7

ABILITY CHECKLIST

Please check the things that you think are **easiest** for this student to do:

☐ Art (drawing/painting) ☐ Dance ☐ Music ☐ Mechanical ☐ Sports ☐ Math ☐ Social ☐ Listening ☐ Talking
☐ Reading ☐ Writing ☐ Other: ______________

Comments:

Please check the things that you think are **hardest** for this student to do:

☐ Art (drawing/painting) ☐ Dance ☐ Music ☐ Mechanical ☐ Sports ☐ Math ☐ Social ☐ Listening ☐ Talking
☐ Reading ☐ Writing ☐ Other: ______________

Comments:

PRIORITY QUESTION

What one thing do you think is most important to help this student do better at school?

Student Language Scale

SLS

TILLS™
TEST OF INTEGRATED LANGUAGE & LITERACY SKILLS™

Nickola Wolf Nelson, Ph.D., CCC-SLP, BCS-CL
Barbara M. Howes, Ph.D., LMSW
Michele A. Anderson, Ph.D., CCC-SLP

This Student Language Scale may be used with the Test of Integrated Language and Literacy Skills™, other assessment tests, or as a stand-alone measure to gather multiple perspectives on a student's language/literacy abilities and other skills.

Student's name: ______________________________ Grade: __________ Date: __________

Person responding: ☐ General education teacher ☐ Special education teacher ☐ Other: ______________
☐ Student ☐ Parent/guardian

RATING SCALE

Compared with other students of the same age, circle the number to show how good this student is at…	**Not good**						**Very good**
1. Understanding school vocabulary words	1	2	3	4	5	6	7
2. Using school vocabulary words when talking	1	2	3	4	5	6	7
3. Figuring out new words when reading	1	2	3	4	5	6	7
4. Spelling words correctly when writing	1	2	3	4	5	6	7
5. Understanding a story when listening	1	2	3	4	5	6	7
6. Telling a story that makes sense	1	2	3	4	5	6	7
7. Understanding a story when reading	1	2	3	4	5	6	7
8. Writing a story that makes sense	1	2	3	4	5	6	7
9. Following spoken directions	1	2	3	4	5	6	7
10. Being organized about schoolwork	1	2	3	4	5	6	7
11. Paying attention in school	1	2	3	4	5	6	7
12. Interacting socially with other students	1	2	3	4	5	6	7

ABILITY CHECKLIST

Please check the things that you think are **easiest** for this student to do:

☐ Art (drawing/painting) ☐ Dance ☐ Music ☐ Mechanical ☐ Sports ☐ Math ☐ Social ☐ Listening ☐ Talking
☐ Reading ☐ Writing ☐ Other: ______________

Comments:

Please check the things that you think are **hardest** for this student to do:

☐ Art (drawing/painting) ☐ Dance ☐ Music ☐ Mechanical ☐ Sports ☐ Math ☐ Social ☐ Listening ☐ Talking
☐ Reading ☐ Writing ☐ Other: ______________

Comments:

PRIORITY QUESTION

What one thing do you think is most important to help this student do better at school?

P2010301

Student Language Scale

SLS

TILLS™ TEST OF INTEGRATED LANGUAGE & LITERACY SKILLS™

Nickola Wolf Nelson, Ph.D., CCC-SLP, BCS-CL
Barbara M. Howes, Ph.D., LMSW
Michele A. Anderson, Ph.D., CCC-SLP

This Student Language Scale may be used with the Test of Integrated Language and Literacy Skills™, other assessment tests, or as a stand-alone measure to gather multiple perspectives on a student's language/literacy abilities and other skills.

Student's name: ______________________ Grade: ________ Date: ________

Person responding: ☐ General education teacher ☐ Special education teacher ☐ Other: ____________
☐ Student ☐ Parent/guardian

RATING SCALE

Compared with other students of the same age, circle the number to show how good this student is at...	**Not good**						**Very good**
1. Understanding school vocabulary words	1	2	3	4	5	6	7
2. Using school vocabulary words when talking	1	2	3	4	5	6	7
3. Figuring out new words when reading	1	2	3	4	5	6	7
4. Spelling words correctly when writing	1	2	3	4	5	6	7
5. Understanding a story when listening	1	2	3	4	5	6	7
6. Telling a story that makes sense	1	2	3	4	5	6	7
7. Understanding a story when reading	1	2	3	4	5	6	7
8. Writing a story that makes sense	1	2	3	4	5	6	7
9. Following spoken directions	1	2	3	4	5	6	7
10. Being organized about schoolwork	1	2	3	4	5	6	7
11. Paying attention in school	1	2	3	4	5	6	7
12. Interacting socially with other students	1	2	3	4	5	6	7

ABILITY CHECKLIST

Please check the things that you think are **easiest** for this student to do:

☐ Art (drawing/painting) ☐ Dance ☐ Music ☐ Mechanical ☐ Sports ☐ Math ☐ Social ☐ Listening ☐ Talking
☐ Reading ☐ Writing ☐ Other: ____________

Comments:

Please check the things that you think are **hardest** for this student to do:

☐ Art (drawing/painting) ☐ Dance ☐ Music ☐ Mechanical ☐ Sports ☐ Math ☐ Social ☐ Listening ☐ Talking
☐ Reading ☐ Writing ☐ Other: ____________

Comments:

PRIORITY QUESTION

What one thing do you think is most important to help this student do better at school?

P2010301

Student Language Scale

SLS

TILLS™
TEST OF INTEGRATED LANGUAGE & LITERACY SKILLS™

Nickola Wolf Nelson, Ph.D., CCC-SLP, BCS-CL
Barbara M. Howes, Ph.D., LMSW
Michele A. Anderson, Ph.D., CCC-SLP

This Student Language Scale may be used with the Test of Integrated Language and Literacy Skills™, other assessment tests, or as a stand-alone measure to gather multiple perspectives on a student's language/literacy abilities and other skills.

Student's name: ______________________ Grade: __________ Date: __________

Person responding: ☐ General education teacher ☐ Special education teacher ☐ Other: ______________
☐ Student ☐ Parent/guardian

RATING SCALE

Compared with other students of the same age, circle the number to show how good this student is at…	**Not good**						**Very good**
1. Understanding school vocabulary words	1	2	3	4	5	6	7
2. Using school vocabulary words when talking	1	2	3	4	5	6	7
3. Figuring out new words when reading	1	2	3	4	5	6	7
4. Spelling words correctly when writing	1	2	3	4	5	6	7
5. Understanding a story when listening	1	2	3	4	5	6	7
6. Telling a story that makes sense	1	2	3	4	5	6	7
7. Understanding a story when reading	1	2	3	4	5	6	7
8. Writing a story that makes sense	1	2	3	4	5	6	7
9. Following spoken directions	1	2	3	4	5	6	7
10. Being organized about schoolwork	1	2	3	4	5	6	7
11. Paying attention in school	1	2	3	4	5	6	7
12. Interacting socially with other students	1	2	3	4	5	6	7

ABILITY CHECKLIST

Please check the things that you think are **easiest** for this student to do:

☐ Art (drawing/painting) ☐ Dance ☐ Music ☐ Mechanical ☐ Sports ☐ Math ☐ Social ☐ Listening ☐ Talking
☐ Reading ☐ Writing ☐ Other: ______________

Comments:

Please check the things that you think are **hardest** for this student to do:

☐ Art (drawing/painting) ☐ Dance ☐ Music ☐ Mechanical ☐ Sports ☐ Math ☐ Social ☐ Listening ☐ Talking
☐ Reading ☐ Writing ☐ Other: ______________

Comments:

PRIORITY QUESTION

What one thing do you think is most important to help this student do better at school?

Student Language Scale

SLS

TILLS™
TEST OF INTEGRATED LANGUAGE & LITERACY SKILLS™

Nickola Wolf Nelson, Ph.D., CCC-SLP, BCS-CL
Barbara M. Howes, Ph.D., LMSW
Michele A. Anderson, Ph.D., CCC-SLP

This Student Language Scale may be used with the Test of Integrated Language and Literacy Skills™, other assessment tests, or as a stand-alone measure to gather multiple perspectives on a student's language/literacy abilities and other skills.

Student's name: ______________________ Grade: __________ Date: __________

Person responding: ☐ General education teacher ☐ Special education teacher ☐ Other: __________
☐ Student ☐ Parent/guardian

RATING SCALE

Compared with other students of the same age, circle the number to show how good this student is at...	**Not good**						**Very good**
1. Understanding school vocabulary words	1	2	3	4	5	6	7
2. Using school vocabulary words when talking	1	2	3	4	5	6	7
3. Figuring out new words when reading	1	2	3	4	5	6	7
4. Spelling words correctly when writing	1	2	3	4	5	6	7
5. Understanding a story when listening	1	2	3	4	5	6	7
6. Telling a story that makes sense	1	2	3	4	5	6	7
7. Understanding a story when reading	1	2	3	4	5	6	7
8. Writing a story that makes sense	1	2	3	4	5	6	7
9. Following spoken directions	1	2	3	4	5	6	7
10. Being organized about schoolwork	1	2	3	4	5	6	7
11. Paying attention in school	1	2	3	4	5	6	7
12. Interacting socially with other students	1	2	3	4	5	6	7

ABILITY CHECKLIST

Please check the things that you think are **easiest** for this student to do:

☐ Art (drawing/painting) ☐ Dance ☐ Music ☐ Mechanical ☐ Sports ☐ Math ☐ Social ☐ Listening ☐ Talking
☐ Reading ☐ Writing ☐ Other: __________

Comments:

Please check the things that you think are **hardest** for this student to do:

☐ Art (drawing/painting) ☐ Dance ☐ Music ☐ Mechanical ☐ Sports ☐ Math ☐ Social ☐ Listening ☐ Talking
☐ Reading ☐ Writing ☐ Other: __________

Comments:

PRIORITY QUESTION

What one thing do you think is most important to help this student do better at school?

Student Language Scale

SLS

TILS™
TEST OF INTEGRATED LANGUAGE & LITERACY SKILLS™

Nickola Wolf Nelson, Ph.D., CCC-SLP, BCS-CL
Barbara M. Howes, Ph.D., LMSW
Michele A. Anderson, Ph.D., CCC-SLP

This Student Language Scale may be used with the Test of Integrated Language and Literacy Skills™, other assessment tests, or as a stand-alone measure to gather multiple perspectives on a student's language/literacy abilities and other skills.

Student's name: ______________________________ Grade: __________ Date: __________

Person responding: ☐ General education teacher ☐ Special education teacher ☐ Other: __________________
☐ Student ☐ Parent/guardian

RATING SCALE

Compared with other students of the same age, circle the number to show how good this student is at...	**Not good**						**Very good**
1. Understanding school vocabulary words	1	2	3	4	5	6	7
2. Using school vocabulary words when talking	1	2	3	4	5	6	7
3. Figuring out new words when reading	1	2	3	4	5	6	7
4. Spelling words correctly when writing	1	2	3	4	5	6	7
5. Understanding a story when listening	1	2	3	4	5	6	7
6. Telling a story that makes sense	1	2	3	4	5	6	7
7. Understanding a story when reading	1	2	3	4	5	6	7
8. Writing a story that makes sense	1	2	3	4	5	6	7
9. Following spoken directions	1	2	3	4	5	6	7
10. Being organized about schoolwork	1	2	3	4	5	6	7
11. Paying attention in school	1	2	3	4	5	6	7
12. Interacting socially with other students	1	2	3	4	5	6	7

ABILITY CHECKLIST

Please check the things that you think are **easiest** for this student to do:

☐ Art (drawing/painting) ☐ Dance ☐ Music ☐ Mechanical ☐ Sports ☐ Math ☐ Social ☐ Listening ☐ Talking
☐ Reading ☐ Writing ☐ Other: ______________

Comments:

Please check the things that you think are **hardest** for this student to do:

☐ Art (drawing/painting) ☐ Dance ☐ Music ☐ Mechanical ☐ Sports ☐ Math ☐ Social ☐ Listening ☐ Talking
☐ Reading ☐ Writing ☐ Other: ______________

Comments:

PRIORITY QUESTION

What one thing do you think is most important to help this student do better at school?

Student Language Scale

SLS

TILLS™ TEST OF INTEGRATED LANGUAGE & LITERACY SKILLS™

Nickola Wolf Nelson, Ph.D., CCC-SLP, BCS-CL
Barbara M. Howes, Ph.D., LMSW
Michele A. Anderson, Ph.D., CCC-SLP

This Student Language Scale may be used with the Test of Integrated Language and Literacy Skills™, other assessment tests, or as a stand-alone measure to gather multiple perspectives on a student's language/literacy abilities and other skills.

Student's name: ______________________________ Grade: __________ Date: __________

Person responding: ☐ General education teacher ☐ Special education teacher ☐ Other: ______________
☐ Student ☐ Parent/guardian

RATING SCALE

Compared with other students of the same age, circle the number to show how good this student is at...	**Not good**						**Very good**
1. Understanding school vocabulary words	1	2	3	4	5	6	7
2. Using school vocabulary words when talking	1	2	3	4	5	6	7
3. Figuring out new words when reading	1	2	3	4	5	6	7
4. Spelling words correctly when writing	1	2	3	4	5	6	7
5. Understanding a story when listening	1	2	3	4	5	6	7
6. Telling a story that makes sense	1	2	3	4	5	6	7
7. Understanding a story when reading	1	2	3	4	5	6	7
8. Writing a story that makes sense	1	2	3	4	5	6	7
9. Following spoken directions	1	2	3	4	5	6	7
10. Being organized about schoolwork	1	2	3	4	5	6	7
11. Paying attention in school	1	2	3	4	5	6	7
12. Interacting socially with other students	1	2	3	4	5	6	7

ABILITY CHECKLIST

Please check the things that you think are **easiest** for this student to do:

☐ Art (drawing/painting) ☐ Dance ☐ Music ☐ Mechanical ☐ Sports ☐ Math ☐ Social ☐ Listening ☐ Talking
☐ Reading ☐ Writing ☐ Other: ______________

Comments:

Please check the things that you think are **hardest** for this student to do:

☐ Art (drawing/painting) ☐ Dance ☐ Music ☐ Mechanical ☐ Sports ☐ Math ☐ Social ☐ Listening ☐ Talking
☐ Reading ☐ Writing ☐ Other: ______________

Comments:

PRIORITY QUESTION

What one thing do you think is most important to help this student do better at school?

Student Language Scale

SLS

TILLS™
TEST OF INTEGRATED LANGUAGE & LITERACY SKILLS™

Nickola Wolf Nelson, Ph.D., CCC-SLP, BCS-CL
Barbara M. Howes, Ph.D., LMSW
Michele A. Anderson, Ph.D., CCC-SLP

This Student Language Scale may be used with the Test of Integrated Language and Literacy Skills™, other assessment tests, or as a stand-alone measure to gather multiple perspectives on a student's language/literacy abilities and other skills.

Student's name: ______________________ Grade: __________ Date: __________

Person responding: ☐ General education teacher ☐ Special education teacher ☐ Other: __________
☐ Student ☐ Parent/guardian

RATING SCALE

Compared with other students of the same age, circle the number to show how good this student is at...	**Not good**						**Very good**
1. Understanding school vocabulary words	1	2	3	4	5	6	7
2. Using school vocabulary words when talking	1	2	3	4	5	6	7
3. Figuring out new words when reading	1	2	3	4	5	6	7
4. Spelling words correctly when writing	1	2	3	4	5	6	7
5. Understanding a story when listening	1	2	3	4	5	6	7
6. Telling a story that makes sense	1	2	3	4	5	6	7
7. Understanding a story when reading	1	2	3	4	5	6	7
8. Writing a story that makes sense	1	2	3	4	5	6	7
9. Following spoken directions	1	2	3	4	5	6	7
10. Being organized about schoolwork	1	2	3	4	5	6	7
11. Paying attention in school	1	2	3	4	5	6	7
12. Interacting socially with other students	1	2	3	4	5	6	7

ABILITY CHECKLIST

Please check the things that you think are **easiest** for this student to do:

☐ Art (drawing/painting) ☐ Dance ☐ Music ☐ Mechanical ☐ Sports ☐ Math ☐ Social ☐ Listening ☐ Talking
☐ Reading ☐ Writing ☐ Other: __________

Comments:

Please check the things that you think are **hardest** for this student to do:

☐ Art (drawing/painting) ☐ Dance ☐ Music ☐ Mechanical ☐ Sports ☐ Math ☐ Social ☐ Listening ☐ Talking
☐ Reading ☐ Writing ☐ Other: __________

Comments:

PRIORITY QUESTION

What one thing do you think is most important to help this student do better at school?

Student Language Scale

SLS

TILLS™
TEST OF INTEGRATED LANGUAGE & LITERACY SKILLS™

Nickola Wolf Nelson, Ph.D., CCC-SLP, BCS-CL
Barbara M. Howes, Ph.D., LMSW
Michele A. Anderson, Ph.D., CCC-SLP

This Student Language Scale may be used with the Test of Integrated Language and Literacy Skills™, other assessment tests, or as a stand-alone measure to gather multiple perspectives on a student's language/literacy abilities and other skills.

Student's name: ______________________ Grade: __________ Date: __________

Person responding: ☐ General education teacher ☐ Special education teacher ☐ Other: ______________
☐ Student ☐ Parent/guardian

RATING SCALE

Compared with other students of the same age, circle the number to show how good this student is at...	**Not good**						**Very good**
1. Understanding school vocabulary words	1	2	3	4	5	6	7
2. Using school vocabulary words when talking	1	2	3	4	5	6	7
3. Figuring out new words when reading	1	2	3	4	5	6	7
4. Spelling words correctly when writing	1	2	3	4	5	6	7
5. Understanding a story when listening	1	2	3	4	5	6	7
6. Telling a story that makes sense	1	2	3	4	5	6	7
7. Understanding a story when reading	1	2	3	4	5	6	7
8. Writing a story that makes sense	1	2	3	4	5	6	7
9. Following spoken directions	1	2	3	4	5	6	7
10. Being organized about schoolwork	1	2	3	4	5	6	7
11. Paying attention in school	1	2	3	4	5	6	7
12. Interacting socially with other students	1	2	3	4	5	6	7

ABILITY CHECKLIST

Please check the things that you think are **easiest** for this student to do:

☐ Art (drawing/painting) ☐ Dance ☐ Music ☐ Mechanical ☐ Sports ☐ Math ☐ Social ☐ Listening ☐ Talking
☐ Reading ☐ Writing ☐ Other: ______________

Comments:

Please check the things that you think are **hardest** for this student to do:

☐ Art (drawing/painting) ☐ Dance ☐ Music ☐ Mechanical ☐ Sports ☐ Math ☐ Social ☐ Listening ☐ Talking
☐ Reading ☐ Writing ☐ Other: ______________

Comments:

PRIORITY QUESTION

What one thing do you think is most important to help this student do better at school?

Student Language Scale

SLS

TILLS™ TEST OF INTEGRATED LANGUAGE & LITERACY SKILLS™

Nickola Wolf Nelson, Ph.D., CCC-SLP, BCS-CL
Barbara M. Howes, Ph.D., LMSW
Michele A. Anderson, Ph.D., CCC-SLP

This Student Language Scale may be used with the Test of Integrated Language and Literacy Skills™, other assessment tests, or as a stand-alone measure to gather multiple perspectives on a student's language/literacy abilities and other skills.

Student's name: ______________________ Grade: __________ Date: __________

Person responding: ☐ General education teacher ☐ Special education teacher ☐ Other: __________
☐ Student ☐ Parent/guardian

RATING SCALE

Compared with other students of the same age, circle the number to show how good this student is at...	**Not good**						**Very good**
1. Understanding school vocabulary words	1	2	3	4	5	6	7
2. Using school vocabulary words when talking	1	2	3	4	5	6	7
3. Figuring out new words when reading	1	2	3	4	5	6	7
4. Spelling words correctly when writing	1	2	3	4	5	6	7
5. Understanding a story when listening	1	2	3	4	5	6	7
6. Telling a story that makes sense	1	2	3	4	5	6	7
7. Understanding a story when reading	1	2	3	4	5	6	7
8. Writing a story that makes sense	1	2	3	4	5	6	7
9. Following spoken directions	1	2	3	4	5	6	7
10. Being organized about schoolwork	1	2	3	4	5	6	7
11. Paying attention in school	1	2	3	4	5	6	7
12. Interacting socially with other students	1	2	3	4	5	6	7

ABILITY CHECKLIST

Please check the things that you think are **easiest** for this student to do:

☐ Art (drawing/painting) ☐ Dance ☐ Music ☐ Mechanical ☐ Sports ☐ Math ☐ Social ☐ Listening ☐ Talking
☐ Reading ☐ Writing ☐ Other: __________

Comments:

Please check the things that you think are **hardest** for this student to do:

☐ Art (drawing/painting) ☐ Dance ☐ Music ☐ Mechanical ☐ Sports ☐ Math ☐ Social ☐ Listening ☐ Talking
☐ Reading ☐ Writing ☐ Other: __________

Comments:

PRIORITY QUESTION

What one thing do you think is most important to help this student do better at school?

Student Language Scale

SLS

TILLS™ TEST OF INTEGRATED LANGUAGE & LITERACY SKILLS™

Nickola Wolf Nelson, Ph.D., CCC-SLP, BCS-CL
Barbara M. Howes, Ph.D., LMSW
Michele A. Anderson, Ph.D., CCC-SLP

This Student Language Scale may be used with the Test of Integrated Language and Literacy Skills™, other assessment tests, or as a stand-alone measure to gather multiple perspectives on a student's language/literacy abilities and other skills.

Student's name: ______________________ Grade: __________ Date: __________

Person responding: ☐ General education teacher ☐ Special education teacher ☐ Other: ______________
☐ Student ☐ Parent/guardian

RATING SCALE

Compared with other students of the same age, circle the number to show how good this student is at...	**Not good**						**Very good**
1. Understanding school vocabulary words	1	2	3	4	5	6	7
2. Using school vocabulary words when talking	1	2	3	4	5	6	7
3. Figuring out new words when reading	1	2	3	4	5	6	7
4. Spelling words correctly when writing	1	2	3	4	5	6	7
5. Understanding a story when listening	1	2	3	4	5	6	7
6. Telling a story that makes sense	1	2	3	4	5	6	7
7. Understanding a story when reading	1	2	3	4	5	6	7
8. Writing a story that makes sense	1	2	3	4	5	6	7
9. Following spoken directions	1	2	3	4	5	6	7
10. Being organized about schoolwork	1	2	3	4	5	6	7
11. Paying attention in school	1	2	3	4	5	6	7
12. Interacting socially with other students	1	2	3	4	5	6	7

ABILITY CHECKLIST

Please check the things that you think are **easiest** for this student to do:

☐ Art (drawing/painting) ☐ Dance ☐ Music ☐ Mechanical ☐ Sports ☐ Math ☐ Social ☐ Listening ☐ Talking
☐ Reading ☐ Writing ☐ Other: ______________

Comments:

Please check the things that you think are **hardest** for this student to do:

☐ Art (drawing/painting) ☐ Dance ☐ Music ☐ Mechanical ☐ Sports ☐ Math ☐ Social ☐ Listening ☐ Talking
☐ Reading ☐ Writing ☐ Other: ______________

Comments:

PRIORITY QUESTION

What one thing do you think is most important to help this student do better at school?

P2010301

Student Language Scale

SLS

TILS™ TEST OF INTEGRATED LANGUAGE & LITERACY SKILLS™

Nickola Wolf Nelson, Ph.D., CCC-SLP, BCS-CL
Barbara M. Howes, Ph.D., LMSW
Michele A. Anderson, Ph.D., CCC-SLP

This Student Language Scale may be used with the Test of Integrated Language and Literacy Skills™, other assessment tests, or as a stand-alone measure to gather multiple perspectives on a student's language/literacy abilities and other skills.

Student's name: ______________________ Grade: ________ Date: ________

Person responding: ☐ General education teacher ☐ Special education teacher ☐ Other: ____________
☐ Student ☐ Parent/guardian

RATING SCALE

Compared with other students of the same age, circle the number to show how good this student is at...	**Not good**						**Very good**
1. Understanding school vocabulary words	1	2	3	4	5	6	7
2. Using school vocabulary words when talking	1	2	3	4	5	6	7
3. Figuring out new words when reading	1	2	3	4	5	6	7
4. Spelling words correctly when writing	1	2	3	4	5	6	7
5. Understanding a story when listening	1	2	3	4	5	6	7
6. Telling a story that makes sense	1	2	3	4	5	6	7
7. Understanding a story when reading	1	2	3	4	5	6	7
8. Writing a story that makes sense	1	2	3	4	5	6	7
9. Following spoken directions	1	2	3	4	5	6	7
10. Being organized about schoolwork	1	2	3	4	5	6	7
11. Paying attention in school	1	2	3	4	5	6	7
12. Interacting socially with other students	1	2	3	4	5	6	7

ABILITY CHECKLIST

Please check the things that you think are **easiest** for this student to do:

☐ Art (drawing/painting) ☐ Dance ☐ Music ☐ Mechanical ☐ Sports ☐ Math ☐ Social ☐ Listening ☐ Talking
☐ Reading ☐ Writing ☐ Other: ____________

Comments:

Please check the things that you think are **hardest** for this student to do:

☐ Art (drawing/painting) ☐ Dance ☐ Music ☐ Mechanical ☐ Sports ☐ Math ☐ Social ☐ Listening ☐ Talking
☐ Reading ☐ Writing ☐ Other: ____________

Comments:

PRIORITY QUESTION

What one thing do you think is most important to help this student do better at school?

Student Language Scale

SLS

TILLS™
TEST OF INTEGRATED LANGUAGE & LITERACY SKILLS™

Nickola Wolf Nelson, Ph.D., CCC-SLP, BCS-CL
Barbara M. Howes, Ph.D., LMSW
Michele A. Anderson, Ph.D., CCC-SLP

This Student Language Scale may be used with the Test of Integrated Language and Literacy Skills™, other assessment tests, or as a stand-alone measure to gather multiple perspectives on a student's language/literacy abilities and other skills.

Student's name: ______________________ Grade: ________ Date: ________

Person responding: ☐ General education teacher ☐ Special education teacher ☐ Other: ____________
☐ Student ☐ Parent/guardian

RATING SCALE

Compared with other students of the same age, circle the number to show how good this student is at...	**Not good**						**Very good**
1. Understanding school vocabulary words	1	2	3	4	5	6	7
2. Using school vocabulary words when talking	1	2	3	4	5	6	7
3. Figuring out new words when reading	1	2	3	4	5	6	7
4. Spelling words correctly when writing	1	2	3	4	5	6	7
5. Understanding a story when listening	1	2	3	4	5	6	7
6. Telling a story that makes sense	1	2	3	4	5	6	7
7. Understanding a story when reading	1	2	3	4	5	6	7
8. Writing a story that makes sense	1	2	3	4	5	6	7
9. Following spoken directions	1	2	3	4	5	6	7
10. Being organized about schoolwork	1	2	3	4	5	6	7
11. Paying attention in school	1	2	3	4	5	6	7
12. Interacting socially with other students	1	2	3	4	5	6	7

ABILITY CHECKLIST

Please check the things that you think are **easiest** for this student to do:

☐ Art (drawing/painting) ☐ Dance ☐ Music ☐ Mechanical ☐ Sports ☐ Math ☐ Social ☐ Listening ☐ Talking
☐ Reading ☐ Writing ☐ Other: ____________

Comments:

Please check the things that you think are **hardest** for this student to do:

☐ Art (drawing/painting) ☐ Dance ☐ Music ☐ Mechanical ☐ Sports ☐ Math ☐ Social ☐ Listening ☐ Talking
☐ Reading ☐ Writing ☐ Other: ____________

Comments:

PRIORITY QUESTION

What one thing do you think is most important to help this student do better at school?

P2010301

Student Language Scale

SLS

TILLS™
TEST OF INTEGRATED LANGUAGE & LITERACY SKILLS™

Nickola Wolf Nelson, Ph.D., CCC-SLP, BCS-CL
Barbara M. Howes, Ph.D., LMSW
Michele A. Anderson, Ph.D., CCC-SLP

This Student Language Scale may be used with the Test of Integrated Language and Literacy Skills™, other assessment tests, or as a stand-alone measure to gather multiple perspectives on a student's language/literacy abilities and other skills.

Student's name: ______________________ Grade: __________ Date: __________

Person responding: ☐ General education teacher ☐ Special education teacher ☐ Other: __________
☐ Student ☐ Parent/guardian

RATING SCALE

Compared with other students of the same age, circle the number to show how good this student is at...	**Not good**						**Very good**
1. Understanding school vocabulary words	1	2	3	4	5	6	7
2. Using school vocabulary words when talking	1	2	3	4	5	6	7
3. Figuring out new words when reading	1	2	3	4	5	6	7
4. Spelling words correctly when writing	1	2	3	4	5	6	7
5. Understanding a story when listening	1	2	3	4	5	6	7
6. Telling a story that makes sense	1	2	3	4	5	6	7
7. Understanding a story when reading	1	2	3	4	5	6	7
8. Writing a story that makes sense	1	2	3	4	5	6	7
9. Following spoken directions	1	2	3	4	5	6	7
10. Being organized about schoolwork	1	2	3	4	5	6	7
11. Paying attention in school	1	2	3	4	5	6	7
12. Interacting socially with other students	1	2	3	4	5	6	7

ABILITY CHECKLIST

Please check the things that you think are **easiest** for this student to do:

☐ Art (drawing/painting) ☐ Dance ☐ Music ☐ Mechanical ☐ Sports ☐ Math ☐ Social ☐ Listening ☐ Talking
☐ Reading ☐ Writing ☐ Other: __________

Comments:

Please check the things that you think are **hardest** for this student to do:

☐ Art (drawing/painting) ☐ Dance ☐ Music ☐ Mechanical ☐ Sports ☐ Math ☐ Social ☐ Listening ☐ Talking
☐ Reading ☐ Writing ☐ Other: __________

Comments:

PRIORITY QUESTION

What one thing do you think is most important to help this student do better at school?

P2010301

Student Language Scale

SLS

TILLS™
TEST OF INTEGRATED LANGUAGE & LITERACY SKILLS™

Nickola Wolf Nelson, Ph.D., CCC-SLP, BCS-CL
Barbara M. Howes, Ph.D., LMSW
Michele A. Anderson, Ph.D., CCC-SLP

This Student Language Scale may be used with the Test of Integrated Language and Literacy Skills™, other assessment tests, or as a stand-alone measure to gather multiple perspectives on a student's language/literacy abilities and other skills.

Student's name: ______________________ Grade: __________ Date: __________

Person responding: ☐ General education teacher ☐ Special education teacher ☐ Other: __________
☐ Student ☐ Parent/guardian

RATING SCALE

Compared with other students of the same age, circle the number to show how good this student is at...	**Not good**						**Very good**
1. Understanding school vocabulary words	1	2	3	4	5	6	7
2. Using school vocabulary words when talking	1	2	3	4	5	6	7
3. Figuring out new words when reading	1	2	3	4	5	6	7
4. Spelling words correctly when writing	1	2	3	4	5	6	7
5. Understanding a story when listening	1	2	3	4	5	6	7
6. Telling a story that makes sense	1	2	3	4	5	6	7
7. Understanding a story when reading	1	2	3	4	5	6	7
8. Writing a story that makes sense	1	2	3	4	5	6	7
9. Following spoken directions	1	2	3	4	5	6	7
10. Being organized about schoolwork	1	2	3	4	5	6	7
11. Paying attention in school	1	2	3	4	5	6	7
12. Interacting socially with other students	1	2	3	4	5	6	7

ABILITY CHECKLIST

Please check the things that you think are **easiest** for this student to do:

☐ Art (drawing/painting) ☐ Dance ☐ Music ☐ Mechanical ☐ Sports ☐ Math ☐ Social ☐ Listening ☐ Talking
☐ Reading ☐ Writing ☐ Other: __________

Comments:

Please check the things that you think are **hardest** for this student to do:

☐ Art (drawing/painting) ☐ Dance ☐ Music ☐ Mechanical ☐ Sports ☐ Math ☐ Social ☐ Listening ☐ Talking
☐ Reading ☐ Writing ☐ Other: __________

Comments:

PRIORITY QUESTION

What one thing do you think is most important to help this student do better at school?

P2010301

Student Language Scale

SLS

TILLS™
TEST OF INTEGRATED LANGUAGE & LITERACY SKILLS™

Nickola Wolf Nelson, Ph.D., CCC-SLP, BCS-CL
Barbara M. Howes, Ph.D., LMSW
Michele A. Anderson, Ph.D., CCC-SLP

This Student Language Scale may be used with the Test of Integrated Language and Literacy Skills™, other assessment tests, or as a stand-alone measure to gather multiple perspectives on a student's language/literacy abilities and other skills.

Student's name: ______________________ Grade: ________ Date: ________

Person responding: ☐ General education teacher ☐ Special education teacher ☐ Other: ________
☐ Student ☐ Parent/guardian

RATING SCALE

Compared with other students of the same age, circle the number to show how good this student is at...	**Not good**						**Very good**
1. Understanding school vocabulary words	1	2	3	4	5	6	7
2. Using school vocabulary words when talking	1	2	3	4	5	6	7
3. Figuring out new words when reading	1	2	3	4	5	6	7
4. Spelling words correctly when writing	1	2	3	4	5	6	7
5. Understanding a story when listening	1	2	3	4	5	6	7
6. Telling a story that makes sense	1	2	3	4	5	6	7
7. Understanding a story when reading	1	2	3	4	5	6	7
8. Writing a story that makes sense	1	2	3	4	5	6	7
9. Following spoken directions	1	2	3	4	5	6	7
10. Being organized about schoolwork	1	2	3	4	5	6	7
11. Paying attention in school	1	2	3	4	5	6	7
12. Interacting socially with other students	1	2	3	4	5	6	7

ABILITY CHECKLIST

Please check the things that you think are **easiest** for this student to do:

☐ Art (drawing/painting) ☐ Dance ☐ Music ☐ Mechanical ☐ Sports ☐ Math ☐ Social ☐ Listening ☐ Talking
☐ Reading ☐ Writing ☐ Other: ________

Comments:

Please check the things that you think are **hardest** for this student to do:

☐ Art (drawing/painting) ☐ Dance ☐ Music ☐ Mechanical ☐ Sports ☐ Math ☐ Social ☐ Listening ☐ Talking
☐ Reading ☐ Writing ☐ Other: ________

Comments:

PRIORITY QUESTION

What one thing do you think is most important to help this student do better at school?

Student Language Scale

SLS

TILS™ TEST OF INTEGRATED LANGUAGE & LITERACY SKILLS™

Nickola Wolf Nelson, Ph.D., CCC-SLP, BCS-CL
Barbara M. Howes, Ph.D., LMSW
Michele A. Anderson, Ph.D., CCC-SLP

This Student Language Scale may be used with the Test of Integrated Language and Literacy Skills™, other assessment tests, or as a stand-alone measure to gather multiple perspectives on a student's language/literacy abilities and other skills.

Student's name: ______________________________ Grade: __________ Date: __________

Person responding: ☐ General education teacher ☐ Special education teacher ☐ Other: __________________
☐ Student ☐ Parent/guardian

RATING SCALE

Compared with other students of the same age, circle the number to show how good this student is at…	**Not good**						**Very good**
1. Understanding school vocabulary words	1	2	3	4	5	6	7
2. Using school vocabulary words when talking	1	2	3	4	5	6	7
3. Figuring out new words when reading	1	2	3	4	5	6	7
4. Spelling words correctly when writing	1	2	3	4	5	6	7
5. Understanding a story when listening	1	2	3	4	5	6	7
6. Telling a story that makes sense	1	2	3	4	5	6	7
7. Understanding a story when reading	1	2	3	4	5	6	7
8. Writing a story that makes sense	1	2	3	4	5	6	7
9. Following spoken directions	1	2	3	4	5	6	7
10. Being organized about schoolwork	1	2	3	4	5	6	7
11. Paying attention in school	1	2	3	4	5	6	7
12. Interacting socially with other students	1	2	3	4	5	6	7

ABILITY CHECKLIST

Please check the things that you think are **easiest** for this student to do:

☐ Art (drawing/painting) ☐ Dance ☐ Music ☐ Mechanical ☐ Sports ☐ Math ☐ Social ☐ Listening ☐ Talking
☐ Reading ☐ Writing ☐ Other: ______________

Comments:

Please check the things that you think are **hardest** for this student to do:

☐ Art (drawing/painting) ☐ Dance ☐ Music ☐ Mechanical ☐ Sports ☐ Math ☐ Social ☐ Listening ☐ Talking
☐ Reading ☐ Writing ☐ Other: ______________

Comments:

PRIORITY QUESTION

What one thing do you think is most important to help this student do better at school?

P2010301

Student Language Scale

SLS

TILLS™
TEST OF INTEGRATED LANGUAGE & LITERACY SKILLS™

Nickola Wolf Nelson, Ph.D., CCC-SLP, BCS-CL
Barbara M. Howes, Ph.D., LMSW
Michele A. Anderson, Ph.D., CCC-SLP

This Student Language Scale may be used with the Test of Integrated Language and Literacy Skills™, other assessment tests, or as a stand-alone measure to gather multiple perspectives on a student's language/literacy abilities and other skills.

Student's name: ______________________ Grade: __________ Date: __________

Person responding: ☐ General education teacher ☐ Special education teacher ☐ Other: __________
☐ Student ☐ Parent/guardian

RATING SCALE

Compared with other students of the same age, circle the number to show how good this student is at...	**Not good**						**Very good**
1. Understanding school vocabulary words	1	2	3	4	5	6	7
2. Using school vocabulary words when talking	1	2	3	4	5	6	7
3. Figuring out new words when reading	1	2	3	4	5	6	7
4. Spelling words correctly when writing	1	2	3	4	5	6	7
5. Understanding a story when listening	1	2	3	4	5	6	7
6. Telling a story that makes sense	1	2	3	4	5	6	7
7. Understanding a story when reading	1	2	3	4	5	6	7
8. Writing a story that makes sense	1	2	3	4	5	6	7
9. Following spoken directions	1	2	3	4	5	6	7
10. Being organized about schoolwork	1	2	3	4	5	6	7
11. Paying attention in school	1	2	3	4	5	6	7
12. Interacting socially with other students	1	2	3	4	5	6	7

ABILITY CHECKLIST

Please check the things that you think are **easiest** for this student to do:

☐ Art (drawing/painting) ☐ Dance ☐ Music ☐ Mechanical ☐ Sports ☐ Math ☐ Social ☐ Listening ☐ Talking
☐ Reading ☐ Writing ☐ Other: __________

Comments:

Please check the things that you think are **hardest** for this student to do:

☐ Art (drawing/painting) ☐ Dance ☐ Music ☐ Mechanical ☐ Sports ☐ Math ☐ Social ☐ Listening ☐ Talking
☐ Reading ☐ Writing ☐ Other: __________

Comments:

PRIORITY QUESTION

What one thing do you think is most important to help this student do better at school?

P2010301

Student Language Scale

SLS

TILLS™ TEST OF INTEGRATED LANGUAGE & LITERACY SKILLS™

Nickola Wolf Nelson, Ph.D., CCC-SLP, BCS-CL
Barbara M. Howes, Ph.D., LMSW
Michele A. Anderson, Ph.D., CCC-SLP

This Student Language Scale may be used with the Test of Integrated Language and Literacy Skills™, other assessment tests, or as a stand-alone measure to gather multiple perspectives on a student's language/literacy abilities and other skills.

Student's name: ______________________ Grade: __________ Date: __________

Person responding: ☐ General education teacher ☐ Special education teacher ☐ Other: __________
☐ Student ☐ Parent/guardian

RATING SCALE

Compared with other students of the same age, circle the number to show how good this student is at...	**Not good**						**Very good**
1. Understanding school vocabulary words	1	2	3	4	5	6	7
2. Using school vocabulary words when talking	1	2	3	4	5	6	7
3. Figuring out new words when reading	1	2	3	4	5	6	7
4. Spelling words correctly when writing	1	2	3	4	5	6	7
5. Understanding a story when listening	1	2	3	4	5	6	7
6. Telling a story that makes sense	1	2	3	4	5	6	7
7. Understanding a story when reading	1	2	3	4	5	6	7
8. Writing a story that makes sense	1	2	3	4	5	6	7
9. Following spoken directions	1	2	3	4	5	6	7
10. Being organized about schoolwork	1	2	3	4	5	6	7
11. Paying attention in school	1	2	3	4	5	6	7
12. Interacting socially with other students	1	2	3	4	5	6	7

ABILITY CHECKLIST

Please check the things that you think are **easiest** for this student to do:

☐ Art (drawing/painting) ☐ Dance ☐ Music ☐ Mechanical ☐ Sports ☐ Math ☐ Social ☐ Listening ☐ Talking
☐ Reading ☐ Writing ☐ Other: __________

Comments:

Please check the things that you think are **hardest** for this student to do:

☐ Art (drawing/painting) ☐ Dance ☐ Music ☐ Mechanical ☐ Sports ☐ Math ☐ Social ☐ Listening ☐ Talking
☐ Reading ☐ Writing ☐ Other: __________

Comments:

PRIORITY QUESTION

What one thing do you think is most important to help this student do better at school?

Student Language Scale

SLS

TILLS™
TEST OF INTEGRATED LANGUAGE & LITERACY SKILLS™

Nickola Wolf Nelson, Ph.D., CCC-SLP, BCS-CL
Barbara M. Howes, Ph.D., LMSW
Michele A. Anderson, Ph.D., CCC-SLP

This Student Language Scale may be used with the Test of Integrated Language and Literacy Skills™, other assessment tests, or as a stand-alone measure to gather multiple perspectives on a student's language/literacy abilities and other skills.

Student's name: ______________________ Grade: __________ Date: __________

Person responding: ☐ General education teacher ☐ Special education teacher ☐ Other: __________
☐ Student ☐ Parent/guardian

RATING SCALE

Compared with other students of the same age, circle the number to show how good this student is at...	**Not good**						**Very good**
1. Understanding school vocabulary words	1	2	3	4	5	6	7
2. Using school vocabulary words when talking	1	2	3	4	5	6	7
3. Figuring out new words when reading	1	2	3	4	5	6	7
4. Spelling words correctly when writing	1	2	3	4	5	6	7
5. Understanding a story when listening	1	2	3	4	5	6	7
6. Telling a story that makes sense	1	2	3	4	5	6	7
7. Understanding a story when reading	1	2	3	4	5	6	7
8. Writing a story that makes sense	1	2	3	4	5	6	7
9. Following spoken directions	1	2	3	4	5	6	7
10. Being organized about schoolwork	1	2	3	4	5	6	7
11. Paying attention in school	1	2	3	4	5	6	7
12. Interacting socially with other students	1	2	3	4	5	6	7

ABILITY CHECKLIST

Please check the things that you think are **easiest** for this student to do:

☐ Art (drawing/painting) ☐ Dance ☐ Music ☐ Mechanical ☐ Sports ☐ Math ☐ Social ☐ Listening ☐ Talking
☐ Reading ☐ Writing ☐ Other: __________

Comments:

Please check the things that you think are **hardest** for this student to do:

☐ Art (drawing/painting) ☐ Dance ☐ Music ☐ Mechanical ☐ Sports ☐ Math ☐ Social ☐ Listening ☐ Talking
☐ Reading ☐ Writing ☐ Other: __________

Comments:

PRIORITY QUESTION

What one thing do you think is most important to help this student do better at school?

Student Language Scale

SLS

TILLS™
TEST OF INTEGRATED LANGUAGE & LITERACY SKILLS™

Nickola Wolf Nelson, Ph.D., CCC-SLP, BCS-CL
Barbara M. Howes, Ph.D., LMSW
Michele A. Anderson, Ph.D., CCC-SLP

This Student Language Scale may be used with the Test of Integrated Language and Literacy Skills™, other assessment tests, or as a stand-alone measure to gather multiple perspectives on a student's language/literacy abilities and other skills.

Student's name: ______________________ Grade: __________ Date: __________

Person responding: ☐ General education teacher ☐ Special education teacher ☐ Other: ______________
☐ Student ☐ Parent/guardian

RATING SCALE

Compared with other students of the same age, circle the number to show how good this student is at...	**Not good**						**Very good**
1. Understanding school vocabulary words	1	2	3	4	5	6	7
2. Using school vocabulary words when talking	1	2	3	4	5	6	7
3. Figuring out new words when reading	1	2	3	4	5	6	7
4. Spelling words correctly when writing	1	2	3	4	5	6	7
5. Understanding a story when listening	1	2	3	4	5	6	7
6. Telling a story that makes sense	1	2	3	4	5	6	7
7. Understanding a story when reading	1	2	3	4	5	6	7
8. Writing a story that makes sense	1	2	3	4	5	6	7
9. Following spoken directions	1	2	3	4	5	6	7
10. Being organized about schoolwork	1	2	3	4	5	6	7
11. Paying attention in school	1	2	3	4	5	6	7
12. Interacting socially with other students	1	2	3	4	5	6	7

ABILITY CHECKLIST

Please check the things that you think are **easiest** for this student to do:

☐ Art (drawing/painting) ☐ Dance ☐ Music ☐ Mechanical ☐ Sports ☐ Math ☐ Social ☐ Listening ☐ Talking
☐ Reading ☐ Writing ☐ Other: ______________

Comments:

Please check the things that you think are **hardest** for this student to do:

☐ Art (drawing/painting) ☐ Dance ☐ Music ☐ Mechanical ☐ Sports ☐ Math ☐ Social ☐ Listening ☐ Talking
☐ Reading ☐ Writing ☐ Other: ______________

Comments:

PRIORITY QUESTION

What one thing do you think is most important to help this student do better at school?

Student Language Scale

SLS

TILS™ TEST OF INTEGRATED LANGUAGE & LITERACY SKILLS™

Nickola Wolf Nelson, Ph.D., CCC-SLP, BCS-CL
Barbara M. Howes, Ph.D., LMSW
Michele A. Anderson, Ph.D., CCC-SLP

This Student Language Scale may be used with the Test of Integrated Language and Literacy Skills™, other assessment tests, or as a stand-alone measure to gather multiple perspectives on a student's language/literacy abilities and other skills.

Student's name: ______________________ Grade: __________ Date: __________

Person responding: ☐ General education teacher ☐ Special education teacher ☐ Other: ______________
☐ Student ☐ Parent/guardian

RATING SCALE

Compared with other students of the same age, circle the number to show how good this student is at...	**Not good**						**Very good**
1. Understanding school vocabulary words	1	2	3	4	5	6	7
2. Using school vocabulary words when talking	1	2	3	4	5	6	7
3. Figuring out new words when reading	1	2	3	4	5	6	7
4. Spelling words correctly when writing	1	2	3	4	5	6	7
5. Understanding a story when listening	1	2	3	4	5	6	7
6. Telling a story that makes sense	1	2	3	4	5	6	7
7. Understanding a story when reading	1	2	3	4	5	6	7
8. Writing a story that makes sense	1	2	3	4	5	6	7
9. Following spoken directions	1	2	3	4	5	6	7
10. Being organized about schoolwork	1	2	3	4	5	6	7
11. Paying attention in school	1	2	3	4	5	6	7
12. Interacting socially with other students	1	2	3	4	5	6	7

ABILITY CHECKLIST

Please check the things that you think are **easiest** for this student to do:

☐ Art (drawing/painting) ☐ Dance ☐ Music ☐ Mechanical ☐ Sports ☐ Math ☐ Social ☐ Listening ☐ Talking
☐ Reading ☐ Writing ☐ Other: ______________

Comments:

Please check the things that you think are **hardest** for this student to do:

☐ Art (drawing/painting) ☐ Dance ☐ Music ☐ Mechanical ☐ Sports ☐ Math ☐ Social ☐ Listening ☐ Talking
☐ Reading ☐ Writing ☐ Other: ______________

Comments:

PRIORITY QUESTION

What one thing do you think is most important to help this student do better at school?

Student Language Scale

SLS

TILLS™
TEST OF INTEGRATED LANGUAGE & LITERACY SKILLS™

Nickola Wolf Nelson, Ph.D., CCC-SLP, BCS-CL
Barbara M. Howes, Ph.D., LMSW
Michele A. Anderson, Ph.D., CCC-SLP

This Student Language Scale may be used with the Test of Integrated Language and Literacy Skills™, other assessment tests, or as a stand-alone measure to gather multiple perspectives on a student's language/literacy abilities and other skills.

Student's name: ______________________________ Grade: __________ Date: __________

Person responding: ☐ General education teacher ☐ Special education teacher ☐ Other: ______________
☐ Student ☐ Parent/guardian

RATING SCALE

Compared with other students of the same age, circle the number to show how good this student is at...	**Not good**						**Very good**
1. Understanding school vocabulary words	1	2	3	4	5	6	7
2. Using school vocabulary words when talking	1	2	3	4	5	6	7
3. Figuring out new words when reading	1	2	3	4	5	6	7
4. Spelling words correctly when writing	1	2	3	4	5	6	7
5. Understanding a story when listening	1	2	3	4	5	6	7
6. Telling a story that makes sense	1	2	3	4	5	6	7
7. Understanding a story when reading	1	2	3	4	5	6	7
8. Writing a story that makes sense	1	2	3	4	5	6	7
9. Following spoken directions	1	2	3	4	5	6	7
10. Being organized about schoolwork	1	2	3	4	5	6	7
11. Paying attention in school	1	2	3	4	5	6	7
12. Interacting socially with other students	1	2	3	4	5	6	7

ABILITY CHECKLIST

Please check the things that you think are **easiest** for this student to do:

☐ Art (drawing/painting) ☐ Dance ☐ Music ☐ Mechanical ☐ Sports ☐ Math ☐ Social ☐ Listening ☐ Talking
☐ Reading ☐ Writing ☐ Other: ______________

Comments:

Please check the things that you think are **hardest** for this student to do:

☐ Art (drawing/painting) ☐ Dance ☐ Music ☐ Mechanical ☐ Sports ☐ Math ☐ Social ☐ Listening ☐ Talking
☐ Reading ☐ Writing ☐ Other: ______________

Comments:

PRIORITY QUESTION

What one thing do you think is most important to help this student do better at school?

Student Language Scale

SLS

TILLS™
TEST OF INTEGRATED LANGUAGE & LITERACY SKILLS™

Nickola Wolf Nelson, Ph.D., CCC-SLP, BCS-CL
Barbara M. Howes, Ph.D., LMSW
Michele A. Anderson, Ph.D., CCC-SLP

This Student Language Scale may be used with the Test of Integrated Language and Literacy Skills™, other assessment tests, or as a stand-alone measure to gather multiple perspectives on a student's language/literacy abilities and other skills.

Student's name: ______________________________ Grade: __________ Date: __________

Person responding: ☐ General education teacher ☐ Special education teacher ☐ Other: __________
☐ Student ☐ Parent/guardian

RATING SCALE

Compared with other students of the same age, circle the number to show how good this student is at...	**Not good**						**Very good**
1. Understanding school vocabulary words	1	2	3	4	5	6	7
2. Using school vocabulary words when talking	1	2	3	4	5	6	7
3. Figuring out new words when reading	1	2	3	4	5	6	7
4. Spelling words correctly when writing	1	2	3	4	5	6	7
5. Understanding a story when listening	1	2	3	4	5	6	7
6. Telling a story that makes sense	1	2	3	4	5	6	7
7. Understanding a story when reading	1	2	3	4	5	6	7
8. Writing a story that makes sense	1	2	3	4	5	6	7
9. Following spoken directions	1	2	3	4	5	6	7
10. Being organized about schoolwork	1	2	3	4	5	6	7
11. Paying attention in school	1	2	3	4	5	6	7
12. Interacting socially with other students	1	2	3	4	5	6	7

ABILITY CHECKLIST

Please check the things that you think are **easiest** for this student to do:

☐ Art (drawing/painting) ☐ Dance ☐ Music ☐ Mechanical ☐ Sports ☐ Math ☐ Social ☐ Listening ☐ Talking
☐ Reading ☐ Writing ☐ Other: __________

Comments:

Please check the things that you think are **hardest** for this student to do:

☐ Art (drawing/painting) ☐ Dance ☐ Music ☐ Mechanical ☐ Sports ☐ Math ☐ Social ☐ Listening ☐ Talking
☐ Reading ☐ Writing ☐ Other: __________

Comments:

PRIORITY QUESTION

What one thing do you think is most important to help this student do better at school?